THE NEW
TEACHER'S COMPLETE
REFERENCE GUIDE

THE NEW
TEACHER'S COMPLETE
REFERENCE GUIDE

OR THE

FIRST YEARS ARE THE HARDEST

By

ELLEN HORWITZ FURMAN

Publishers

T. S. DENISON & COMPANY, INC.

Minneapolis

 T. S. DENISON & COMPANY, INC.

Standard Book Number: 513-01271-0
Printed in the United States of America
by The Brings Press
Copyright © MCMLXXIII by T. S. Denison & Co., Inc.
Minneapolis, Minn. 55437

Acknowledgments

The author wishes to express her appreciation to the following people without whose assistance and cooperation this book would never have been written:

Mrs. Marian Hasara

Mrs. Selma Horwitz

Miss Sheila Weisberg

and especially to Dr. Elliot Joseph Furman, Jeffrey Lawrence Furman and David Paul Furman whose patience and understanding made its completion possible.

Preface

A teacher is very similar to an actress. When she is in front of her class, she is on stage and must present her material in a manner which will encourage her audience to react favorably. Instead of applause and standing ovations, she looks for good test results, evidences of pupil-development and occasional smiles. Her job is much more difficult than that of the stage performer because she must learn her lines, or her subject matter thoroughly, and be prepared to expect the unexpected daily. She is unable to select the roles she wants to play because she will be assigned to the class levels, grades and courses the rostering chairman wants her to teach rather than to the ones she prefers or feels most qualified to handle. Furthermore, the teacher's performance must change every period and every day necessitating her to devise new materials to constantly excite her captive audiences. Her material is not written in advance for her by a well-paid professional. She must prepare her lessons and adapt them to the audiences who, in many cases, would prefer to be in any place other than a school room. Like the actress, her "show must go on" in the face of fire drills, late assemblies, power failures, supply shortages, bomb threats, walkouts and flu epidemics.

Each year, urban school systems lose hundreds of potentially successful teachers because the first year of teaching is so overwhelmingly difficult that many novices drop out of the profession before discovering that the rewards far surpass the exhaustion, depression and feelings of defeat.

Those who have the tenacity to remain in the classroom until their second and third years find that their classroom experiences become progressively less difficult and increasingly more rewarding. This is because time and experience teaches them that there are practices which not only simplify the educational process and enable teachers to endure the daily confrontations with pupils but, at the same time, make it relatively easy for the teacher to be confident, satisfied and successful as an educator. Most third and fourth-year teachers can be overheard consoling beginners each semester by lamenting that if they only knew in their early years in the classroom what they have come to realize as a result of their experiences, they would not have cried and contemplated suicide or running away as frequently as they did. This book represents a composite of those practices upon which the experienced teacher relies as a matter of habit. After several terms in the classroom, sound educational practices become almost second nature to the effective teacher and she is capable of handling almost any situation which arises without panicking. Until the new teacher reaches that point, however, she needs a source to which she can refer to discover how to handle the daily school problems which, in the beginning of her career, seem almost insurmountable.

Most college graduates enter the classroom with the proverbial list of things they will never do once they become educators. These things include vows such as never embarrassing students, boring classes, or appearing aloof and unreachable. When examining their first year in retrospect, most find that they not only committed the offenses they were so anxious to avoid but added a few unpleasant practices they had not thought of before. This can be attributed, in large part, to the fact that most college graduates come equipped with a long list of practical *don'ts* and theoretical *dos*. What they need are a few more positive workable concepts. This book contains the practical classroom teaching techniques they need to know.

The chapters of this text offer suggestions for meeting the daily situations encountered by all new teachers and many experienced ones. The ideas expressed here must be viewed as suggestions which need to be adapted to the maturity and the intellectual and cultural backgrounds of your pupils. While the attempt has been made to tell you everything you must know about teaching, the classroom is such a dynamic place that no one can ever predict every situation which might arise. Should the totally unexpected occur, remain calm and try to rely on your maturity, intelligence and sense of humor to find an acceptable solution to the problem. Keep in mind the words of French scientist Louis Pasteur who said that "chance favors the prepared mind." The more you know about the problems which are likely to occur in the classroom and in interactions with students and colleagues, the better prepared you will be to handle these situations when the unexpected does happen. In confrontations with pupils, keep telling yourself that even if they're bigger than you are, you're older and more experienced than they are. That should count for something. Good luck and try to remember that as your years in the classroom increase, the tensions and uncertainties are replaced by accomplishments and countless rewards.

The female pronoun will be used to indicate the teacher, and the male pronoun to refer to the student only for purposes of clarity and differentiation.

Contents

Chapter One
Activities for the Opening Days of School 13

Chapter Two
Classroom Management Procedures 25

Chapter Three
Classroom Control 33

Chapter Four
Discipline 55

Chapter Five
Effective Lesson Planning 67

Chapter Six
Room Decoration 87

Chapter Seven
Individual Differences 93

Chapter Eight
Every Teacher as a Reading Teacher 99

Chapter Nine
Techniques for Teaching Slow Learners 105

Chapter Ten
Handling Interpersonal Relationships 119

Chapter Eleven
Testing and Grading Procedures 159

Chapter Twelve
Supportive Services Available to the Teacher 179

Chapter Thirteen
Problems in Education 197

Chapter Fourteen
Innovations in Education 217

Chapter Fifteen
Problems for Consideration 237

Epilogue 243

Chapter One

Activities for the Opening Days of School

The new teacher's thoughts about the initial meetings with prospective pupils are fraught with fears and anxieties. This is not only natural and common but is a very good sign that the teacher is concerned about her role and is anxious to succeed. Even the most experienced educators will confess to having "opening day jitters." This can be attributed to their realization of the importance of the first meetings between students and teacher. Meetings between strangers are usually uncomfortable. The discomfort in teaching situations is compounded by the fact that the individuals involved are confined to a classroom for a definite time period and are forced to interact with each other. Both teacher and students are aware that they are being evaluated and this only serves to increase the tension.

Secondary school teachers do not have the option open to college instructors of dismissing their pupils after they have finished their introductory remarks. They must keep the students in the classrooms until the allotted time period, usually between forty and fifty minutes, has expired. Attempting to fill entire class sessions with meaningful activities while trying to make favorable impressions upon students with whom the teacher must meet for an entire semester is a difficult and demanding task. While the teacher must acknowledge that she is not in the classroom to win a popularity contest or cement new friendships, it is vitally important that the initial encounters be pleasant and profitable for the parties involved. These initial sessions set the tone for the entire term. Unsatisfactory first meetings can, of course, be overcome, but it is much to the educator's advantage to begin the semester with positive feelings on both sides rather than trying to reconstruct positive and meaningful relationships later in the term. All teachers can remember how easily they judged the quality of their instructors at the beginnings of the school years when they were students. They can recall, certainly, frantic meetings with friends after classes ended to discuss what teachers were "good" and which were "bad" and to devise plans to avoid the "bad" ones by dropping courses and having schedules altered.

To avoid being one of the "bad" teachers, the educator must plan a definite program before entering the classroom to meet the pupils for the first time. You must have sufficient activities devised to keep your classes occupied during the entire period they are with you on those days before materials and books have been distributed and assignments completed. If the class is not kept busy, the students become noisy, rowdy and destructive. Paper, pens, clips and fasteners, books, lunches and eventually chairs and students are thrown around the room and out of the windows if the students are not occupied with meaningful activities. This sets the pattern for the entire semester and it will be almost impossible to have them settle into organized work patterns once they have tasted the total freedom of chaos.

The following activities are suggested as methods for keeping your classes busy during those vitally important first days before the actual classwork can begin. These tasks are not designed merely as "busy work" to keep the pupils occupied. Even the slowest and most immature students can easily detect those assignments given primarily to keep them from bothering their teachers. They resent both the chores and the people who assigned them. The suggestions which follow are for jobs which should be done if the term's work is to be accomplished smoothly. They are activities which

14

require a minimum of teacher preparation and do not rely on students' prior learning experiences.

Use your own discretion in deleting those suggestions which are not suitable to your pupils' intellectual and emotional capabilities or to their grade levels. As a new teacher, you can determine what these capabilities are on the basis of school records, pupils' course selection, grade levels and information from more experienced teachers. Being in the classroom for a few minutes will also give the perceptive educator an insight into her pupils' abilities and levels of maturity.

GIVE THE PUPILS PERMANENT SEATS

It is very wise to have seating charts prepared for the first day of class or as soon thereafter as possible. A seating chart is a block diagram showing the number and location of useable desks in your classroom. Into the blocks insert the names of the pupils listed on the official roll sheets you will be given for each of the sections you teach. Lists of the students in your sections are usually available the day before classes begin or early in the morning on the first day of school. If such a list is not available or has been lost, have the students sign a blank sheet of paper on your first meeting. Then prepare the seating chart for the second class session.

When time permits, make an extra copy of your charts. Keep one always available in your desk or on file with your department chairman or principal for use by your substitute in case of absence. Check your charts frequently to keep them up to date. Record all additions and deletions and make note of all changes in seating arrangements as they occur. Enabling a substitute to call your pupils by name will help her to maintain control in your absence. This, in turn, will make it easier for you to maintain order when you return.

Minor changes in the seating charts can be made to provide for enrollment additions and deletions as they occur. Last minute alterations can be made as you encounter individual problems in behavior or physical disabilities such as poor eyesight and hearing.

Giving seats to thirty or forty pupils at one time is not as simple a task as it sounds. The more organized and structured the procedure is that you follow, the less likely you are to have a chaotic situation develop. A simple way to seat the pupils is to first allow the class to enter and select seats randomly. Once the pupils are quiet, have the students in one row of chairs only vacate their seats. Do not begin before you have total silence. Instruct them to stand quietly in the back of the room. Read the names of the pupils belonging in the empty row. Have only those students whose names you've read move into their permanent seats while the remainder of the class is seated. Then have the students move out of the second row and follow the same procedure with each subsequent row until all of the names have been called.

Having your seating charts prepared in advance and waiting until the class is quiet and attentive before assigning seats or allowing the pupils to move will enable you to complete the entire procedure in no more than five or ten minutes. It will also prevent the chaotic "who me?" game in which students get great delight from not hearing their names called over the din of their peers' voices. It also avoids the "tapping on the head or stepping on the neighbor's foot" syndromes which occur frequently in the anonymity of mass movements for seat changing purposes.

INTRODUCE YOURSELF TO THE CLASS

Once the pupils have been seated and are quiet and attentive, tell them about youself. Most students are very anxious to know about their teachers as "real people" rather than as the aloof authoritarian figures they are used to seeing in front of them each day. The amount and kind of things you select to relate to the class should be guided by the social and intellectual maturity of the group as well as by your own common sense. Your aim should be to enable the students to view you as a thinking, feeling human being who is interested in their needs and ambitions without lowering yourself to their maturity levels or becoming too personal and undermining your authority as the classroom leader.

Information on the number of people in your immediate family, the sex of your children, your hobbies, musical preferences and unusual places you have lived or visited as well as other jobs you have held are "safe" areas of your background which are usually of interest to pupils. Your sex life, weight, clothing size, financial situation, opinions of school or administrative policies, and feelings toward other teachers are not advisable topics for classroom discussion.

More intellectual subjects such as your tastes in literature and opinions of current events can be discussed later in the semester if they become relevant to the context of the course and after the term has progressed far enough for you to determine your students' ability to cope with more sophisticated material.

More advanced students will be interested in knowing about your educational background. They will be concerned about the schools you have attended as well as your areas of specialization.

PREPARE THE STUDENTS FOR THE TERM'S WORK

Begin by telling the pupils how you expect them to behave in your classroom. Make explicit the rules and regulations you expect them to follow. Before announcing these rules to the class check with an experienced teacher or administrator to be certain that your requirements and punishments for infringements are not contrary to established school policies. When you discuss these rules, and the consequences for breaking them, your manner must not reflect a challenge because in every class you are certain to find many students willing to accept the challenge. State your behavioral expectations in a tone which indicates that you feel that you are merely reminding the "few" pupils in the class who might be tempted to err in their deportment about the acceptable standards of behavior in your classroom rather than one which insults the integrity of your pupils or dares them to test your ability to carry out your threats.

Never make the mistake of assuming that the pupils will automatically display the kind of behavior you want them to. They must be told what procedures you require them to follow in order to be excused from your class. They must be reminded that you expect them to attend class daily unless they are excused for an acceptable reason such as illness. The circumstances under which they will be permitted to go to the drinking fountain or lavatories must be discussed. Inane as this may sound to the college graduate, when the weather gets warm or the work becomes difficult, you must be prepared for a rush on requests for hall passes and early dismissal notes. Establishing a clear policy at the beginning of the term which precludes all absences except those for the most dire emergencies will offset potential problems later in the year.

A warning against late arrivals to class will prevent loitering in the halls and interruptions by latecomers once the classwork has begun.

In addition to discussing deportment, the teacher should prepare the pupils for what they must achieve scholastically. Let the students know what work they must do in order to pass the course and what they must do in order to excel. Establish standards for the various grades and tell them what they must do in order to meet your standards. Clarify basic standards such as penalties for late work, sloppiness and failure to complete the assignment in its entirety. Be certain that the students know how much time you require them to spend outside of class in language laboratories, at conferences, in the library doing research and going to cultural centers if these activities are applicable to your subject area.

If your list of rules, standards and requirements is a long one or a difficult one to remember, it would be to your advantage and that of your students to mimeograph the list before the class and give a copy to each pupil. Go over each item orally and explain it in enough detail so that you are convinced that the entire class understands what you are going to require of them. In this way no student will be justified in saying later that "no one told me that" about your requirements.

After conveying the above information, you can deal with the more specific informational areas you intend to cover. Give the class a brief synopsis of the course including the skills you hope they will master. List all the supplies and books they will have to supply themselves. Slower students need to be reminded repeatedly that they have to bring pencils, pens, writing paper and textbooks to class daily. They tend to forget these tools more often than they remember them and almost daily prodding is needed. If you overlook this important requirement, you take the risk of having the majority of your students sitting idly or annoying classmates because they are not able to participate in the lesson you are teaching and have nothing else to do other than distracting their peers.

If the students will have to purchase supplies in addition to items normally required, it would be wise to let them know about these as early in the semester as possible so they can save the money gradually. If you want the class to buy theater tickets, drawing supplies, slide rules or paperback books in the third month of the term, tell them about it early in the year and remind them about it frequently thereafter.

When the students have been told of what the basic course is to consist, ask them if there is anything they would like to do or learn in addition to what you've already discussed. It is possible that the class will have nothing to add to what you've forecasted, but there is a chance that some pupils might suggest a book they'd like to read or a trip they'd like to take which could enhance the term's work. Even if their suggestions are not feasible, what they say will give you an insight into the interests of your pupils which you might be able to satisfy in some types of related activity.

Although some classes will have nothing to suggest, the mere fact that you took the time to express an interest in their desires will help to build a positive relationship between you and the class by virtue of the fact that you indicated an interest and willingness to listen to them. This is something to which students react very favorably even though they might not express their appreciation openly.

SET UP CLASSROOM PROCEDURES AND ASSIGN PUPILS TO HELP YOU WITH CLASSROOM DUTIES

Depending upon the maturity of your classes, you might ask the pupils to suggest some workable procedures for getting the annoying, time-consuming chores such as distributing and collecting textbooks, papers and supplies accomplished quickly without causing disruptions or chaos. Building upon pupils' suggestions will help to keep a democratic, cooperative atmosphere in the classroom.

The opening classes afford you the time to assign pupils to perform the many annoying little tasks which are done in the daily normal functioning of the classroom. These duties can be handled easily by pupils of all intelligence levels so the new teacher need not be concerned about delegating these jobs to pupils she does not know very well. If time proves that you have erred by giving a student a job he can't handle, the situation is easily rectified by transferring the responsibilities to another class member. Having the pupils perform certain duties serves the dual function of giving the class the opportunity to assume some of the responsibility for the smooth functioning of the classroom while freeing the teacher to devote more time to teaching. The following tasks are those most commonly and most effectively handled by pupils:

Erasing and/or washing the boards before and after each class

Putting movable chairs and desks into their proper places

Collecting and distributing supplies and materials

Straightening closets and shelves where materials are stored

Delivering messages to other classrooms and offices

Posting materials on bulletin boards

Adjusting windows, shades and lights

Keeping permanent records of class assignments for reference by absentees and new admissions to class

Greeting guests and visitors

ADMINISTER DIAGNOSTIC TESTS

Diagnostic tests will help you to establish and evaluate the abilities and previous learning experiences of your students. It is important that these tests be administered in the opening week of school so that you can determine the achievement levels and capabilities of class members before you begin presenting the term's work. Nothing loses the interest, attention and cooperation of your pupils faster than attempting to teach them something they already know or requiring them to deal with materials which are far beyond their levels of comprehension.

Students will often tell a teacher, especially a novice who introduces a new book or assignment, that "we know that already" or "we learned that last term." Sometimes they are correct. They do know the work you are presenting and reteaching it would only waste your time and theirs. Other times, the pupils really think they know the material when they don't. In other instances, the class doesn't want to learn what you are presenting and will try to dissuade you by professing to have studied the material previously. The only way to determine with any reliability how much the students actually do know is to test them yourself.

These diagnostic tests can take various forms. They might be oral answers to questions which require the repetition or coalition of facts or they can be short ans,.er and

21

essay written examinations or drills. Whatever form you select, it is a good principle to begin with questions that are at least three grade levels below that which you are teaching. Begin with the most elementary material and progress gradually to those skills which are several grades above the point at which you hope to begin teaching. The results of the tests will not only indicate the overall ability of the class but will show the teacher which students are at the upper and lower extremes of the ability scales. This will enable her to make the necessary provisions to provide for their individual needs. The results will also help to locate any students who have been rostered into your section incorrectly. Pupils with far greater or lesser ability than the rest of the section can be reassigned before the term progresses too far for them to adapt to a new group.

HAVE THE STUDENTS TELL YOU
ABOUT THEMSELVES

Since the students have listened to you tell them about yourself, it would only be fair and very profitable for you to listen to them speak about themselves. If the tone of the class permits, and it should if you have been keeping the students quiet, respectful and occupied, ask the pupils to introduce themselves to you and to their classmates. Suggest that they talk about their interests, ambitions, family size, cities in which they've lived, hobbies, and movie, television and music preferences. It would be wise to allow them to speak from their seats rather than asking them to stand or come to the front of the room. As most students are very shy in front of their peers, the less conspicuous they feel, the more likely they are to cooperate. Any pupil who refuses to speak should not be chastised or embarrassed. Such an act would totally destroy any possibility of obtaining a satisfactory teacher-pupil relationship.

In addition to improving the rapport between the class and the teacher, the information the pupils offer and the manner in which it is given gives the educator an insight into individual differences in speech patterns, verbal abilities, interests and intelligence levels. This information is invaluable when you are structuring future lessons and in helping you to cope with the students as individuals.

The new teacher will realize as the term speeds on toward summer vacation that every period is important. This includes the first class sessions also. Use these periods wisely to acquaint your pupils with you, your standards and your expectations. Likewise, you should learn as much about them as you possibly can so that you are able to begin the year's work in a positive direction.

Chapter Two

Classroom Management Procedures

One cardinal principle of education which all new teachers must recognize and accept is that learning cannot take place in a chaotic situation. This does not mean that an educator must maintain a noiseless, inanimate classroom or that the students must perform like robots. It does mean, however, that the teacher must be in total control of classroom activities at all times. Being aware of what forty students are doing at any given moment is a gargantuan task but is a skill teachers develop with time and experience. Until you acquire this art, the more organized and quiet your classroom is the more likely you are to remain in complete control of your pupils and their activities.

If students are to learn, they must be able to see and hear what is being presented to them by their classmates and teacher. The more practiced an educator is, the more qualified she becomes to distinguish between constructive and destructive noise. Activity for activity's sake alone accomplishes nothing. For this reason, the novice would do well to try to keep the class working as quietly as possible in the beginning of the year until a combination of instinct and experience enables her to differentiate between the various kinds of classroom noise and the reasons for the student activity. She should also wait to exercise leniency and latitude in lesson planning until she is able to return the class from a noisy activity to a silent one instantly if she has to.

Classroom noises and disruptions can be kept at a minimum if procedures are well-organized and clear at the beginning of the term. An organized pattern for each class period's activities should also be established. Despite the initial rebellion against rules and organization, the majority of your students, many of whom come from confused, chaotic home environments, look forward to the security they find in a stable classroom situation. This is particularly true in the case of slower and more immature pupils who find adaptation to change most difficult and uncomfortable.

Students can be of great assistance in getting class procedures to function smoothly and the wise teacher uses her pupil-resources to her best advantage. The duties that class members can handle without much difficulty were listed in the first chapter. The reasons for delegating these particular responsibilities are obvious. If a pupil has been assigned to take care of erasing the boards before class begins, you can start your instruction as soon as the class arrives and is seated. While student helpers distribute books, you can check attendance.

Collecting and distributing materials can turn into book-throwing, pencil-jabbing free-for-alls if they are not handled efficiently. Appoint two or three responsible students to distribute supplies. Instruct them to count the materials before and after distribution. You should also keep your own record of the amount and number of your supplies as the school will hold you ultimately responsible for their loss or destruction. Permit your assistants to give supplies or papers to only one row of students at a time. Do not allow the class to pass materials while people are noisy or talking. Distribute books to one row at a time and collect them the same way. Have the distributors give enough supplies to the first person in each row and allow them to pass them to the students behind them. This will save time and prevent pupils from having to walk up and down aisles where they are liable to be pinched, pushed or tripped. Be certain that they give the exact number of supplies to the people in the front seats so that the last students in each row do not have the opportunity to wail about being omitted. The fewer students you have out of their seats at a time the better it is. Distributing supplies in the manner just suggested prevents thirty pupils from jamming the book or supply closet at the same moment and prevents the problems which occur when they do.

Most schools publish daily newsletters with announcements for the student body and faculty. One helper can be assigned to post the announcement sheet on the bulletin board daily so that his classmates can check the announcements as often as they need to refer to them. Aides can be delegated to take care of bulletin board decorations. Most classrooms have enough bulletin board space so that some areas can be designated for the development of content units your classes are studying and others can be delegated for more general purposes such as advertising school activities or celebrating national and civic events and holidays. Having students who are responsible for maintaining existing displays in good repair will prevent loosely-hanging papers and torn pictures from distracting the attention of your class. Unkempt bulletin boards also invite graffiti and destruction and are generally undesirable for a variety of obvious reasons.

It is wise to have one pupil selected to deliver messages. This prevents hand-waving and pleading every time someone must be sent from the room. If you wish, you can change messengers every few weeks using the duty as a reward for good behavior or scholastic achievement. Be certain to select someone who is likely to return to your classroom immediately after his job has been completed rather than going to the lunchroom for a snack or stopping off for a smoke on his return trip.

Adjusting open window levels and keeping shades even is a more important job than a new teacher might imagine. Although it may seem unimportant to an inexperienced adult, there is nothing more tempting to students than a window elevated just enough to permit board erasers, books, paper airplanes and fellow students to be thrown through while

the teacher is busy in another section of the room. Dangling window shade cords are also tempting objects from which to dangle pens, lunches and obscene drawings. Uneven window shades are distracting and often invite students to pull on them so they'll rise noisily sending the entire class into gales of forced uproarious laughter.

During your first year of teaching you'll find that you frequently have observers visiting your classroom without invitation or warning. Such unexpected guests can be very distracting. If a student seated near the door has been designated as the official greeter, he or she can quietly give the visitor a book or work sheet and direct them to an empty seat until you are ready to speak to them personally without disturbing the continuity of your lesson. Aside from lessening the immediate pressure on you, this practice will greatly impress your visitors by showing them that you have devised plans in advance to deal with unexpected situations. Furthermore, it may earn a few extra points for you with your department head or principal who is very influential in securing needed supplies, permission for trips and other extra favors.

It will make things easier for you, the students and any one who might be called upon to substitute for you if you assign two reliable students to keep permanent records of the assignments you make. These records can be easily referred to by absentees or someone called upon to handle the class in your absence. This will prevent students from "not knowing something was due" or from occupying your time before and after class with requests to bring them up to date on assignments they missed.

Keep your name, date and time and place of your before-and-after school conference periods posted in a corner of the blackboard. If you have sufficient board space, you might also add a reminder of the next day's homework assignment. This prevents numerous unnecessary questions and serves as a constant reminder to pupils and administrators that you are readily available to help your students whenever they need you.

Be certain that you know and understand the regulations for fire and civil defense drills. Have the procedures for these drills displayed clearly somewhere in the room. Review these rules with the class periodically to be certain they understand them. This will offset panic during drills or actual emergencies.

Always keep an extra supply of paper, chalk, board erasers and pencils in your room. They should be stored in a place which can be locked because they have mysterious ways of disappearing when they are most needed. Having reserves of needed materials will prevent your having to bluff your way through an entire class period without a piece of chalk or board eraser.

The care of textbooks which students are permitted to take home is important because most books must be used by many classes before they are replaced. Require the students to cover their books. They do not have to purchase book covers. Wrapping paper or brown paper bags will protect the books sufficiently. Have the pupils write their names, section numbers, teacher's name and the current term on the inside cover of the book. This will make it easier to recover lost books. Spot check to see that they have followed your instructions.

After distributing those textbooks which the students take home regularly, give out book receipts which must be filled out and returned to you. If the school does not have a standardized form, devise one of your own which you can mimeograph or write on small sheets of paper. This will help you to keep a record of all those students who have books. If a student loses a book, do not give him a replacement until you have checked with your department head or book distribution chairman to learn the procedures for replacing student-lost books. Keep a record of students who do not return texts so that you can account for all the books given to you by the school. The school will hold you responsible for all books assigned to your classes.

Your classroom floors should be kept free of litter. Ask students to remove all debris at the beginning and end of the period. Although it may seem relatively unimportant, litter on the floor is construed by students as an invitation to commit mayhem. Crumpled paper, potato chip bags and gum wrappers plead with students to be thrown, kicked or tossed at classmates and teachers. Litter on the floor is often suggestive of student boredom and rudeness. Although it may not disturb the teacher, many administrators find an unneat classroom floor totally unacceptable and an indication of teacher ineffectiveness.

Preface your request for litter removal with an acknowledgment that you don't think your class or students discarded the trash, but since the next teacher would appreciate a neat classroom, you'd like your pupils to clean all papers from under their desk. More students will respond favorably to this type of request than to demands that they perform janitorial services. One student should carry the wastebasket around the room or the paper from the floor will be hidden in the desks or thrown basketball fashion across the room into the basket.

Getting each class period off to an orderly beginning is easier than trying to regain composure when you want to begin teaching. Requiring your students to enter the room in an orderly fashion results in an organized beginning and prevents potential problems before they begin. Train the students to take their seats by going immediately to the rear of the room as they enter and then coming forward to their assigned places. This need not be done by lining the students outside the classroom door in a group. The procedure can be followed by each individual as he enters the room. This technique is good because it prevents crowds of people from gathering at your desk and obstructing your view of the classroom. Allowing groups to mill around your desk is the best way to encourage the mysterious disappearances of items such as your grade book, teaching notes, pens, pencils and classified messages. Having a clear view of the classroom and students also enables you to detect which pupils are annoying their classmates and to locate trouble spots and prevent outbreaks of violence before they begin.

CONCLUSION

The subjects of classroom management and classroom control are very closely related. This chapter has considered the impersonal organizational procedures which help the class period to progress as smoothly and efficiently as possible. A well-managed classroom is one which is not likely to become chaotic or unruly. Thus, the more smoothly-run the classroom, the less the likelihood that discipline problems will arise. The next chapter considers the interpersonal relationships which must be established in order for the teacher to control the classroom and suggests techniques for administering discipline if her authority is not respected.

Chapter Three

Classroom Control

For many beginning teachers, the concepts of maintaining control and disciplining are synonymous. In reality, they are not the same concept, and progressing under the assumption that they are only serves to alienate students from teachers. Instructors who are able to maintain control without assuming the roles of dictators can prevent the occurrence of situations requiring discipline or punishment.

It cannot be emphasized too strongly that the teacher who obtains control and order in the classroom does not have to become an "omnipotent enforcer" inhumanly enforcing silence and obedience at the cost of warmth, learning, spontaneity and friendship. While all of these are vital to the continuance of meaningful learning experiences, a teacher does not have to sacrifice one to gain the others. Possessing total control means that the effective teacher is aware of what is taking place all over the classroom at all times and is capable of stopping instantly those activities which are contrary to the promotion or continuation of structured learning activities.

The more experienced a teacher is, the more able she is to differentiate between positive and negative classroom activities. The new teacher should make every effort to try to keep the class working as quietly as possible. Reading, drill work, writing compositions and solving problems individually are quiet activities. Using a classroom library, doing group research projects, constructing models and team competition are activities which invite noise and unnecessary activity. Quiet tasks are easier to direct and supervise than noisy ones. Conducting such work will give you time to gain confidence and experience in handling students before you try to control potentially chaotic lessons.

It is easier to keep control of your class if you have order from the outset of the period than if you try to regain it later. The following techniques will help to prevent disorders from arising and therefore will tend to prevent the need for taking disciplinary measures against students later. No matter how organized, effective or experienced a teacher is, the necessity for disciplining pupils will undoubtedly arise and methods for administering punishment will be discussed later in the chapter.

LEARN THE NAMES OF YOUR STUDENTS QUICKLY

It is important for classroom control and for establishing a warm rapport between teacher and students that the educator learn the pupils' names as quickly as possible. Children respond favorably to those who take the time to show an interest in them as individuals. During the opening days of the term you can refer to your seating charts in order to call your pupils by their correct names.

Learning your students' names serves a very practical function. It enables you to speak directly to a student who is causing a disruption or is behaving improperly. Loss of anonymity makes students feel more responsible for their own actions and more apprehensive about being caught doing something wrong. If students know that you know who they are, they become more cooperative.

Being able to call individuals by name prevents students from turning around and pretending not to know whom you're addressing when you point or talk to a sea of faces. You will not have to point into a crowd to tell one student to stop kicking his neighbor, tearing pages from his textbook or making strange clucking noises under his breath. Speaking directly averts the much-enjoyed, greatly overused "who me? no you! no him!" game students like to play. When you can ask John Jones or Mary Smith to stop shooting rubber bands across the room you have saved yourself a lot of explaining and clarifying.

If your seating charts are kept current and accurate you will be able to address students without much difficulty. Feel free to change seats frequently when seating arrangements prove undesirable. When students find their neighbors too distracting or when pupils seated in the back of the room enjoy drumming on their desks and whistling, do not hesitate to separate the pupils or move them to the front of the room where you can watch them more closely.

ARRANGE PERSONAL CONFERENCES
WITH STUDENTS

Arrange personal conferences with students who give evidence of becoming serious troublemakers. Many problems can be solved or averted through personal contacts made by the teacher. Asking the student what is bothering him, why he isn't doing the assigned work, why he is having trouble concentrating or why he and his neighbor are unable to get along with each other, can give you an insight into the problem and its possible solution. Even if the pupil or pupils cannot answer your questions, and, in many instances, they cannot because they don't really know why they behave or misbehave the way they do, they will certainly respond more favorably to your private inquiry than they would to a public castigation before their peers.

When you are talking to the pupil, it is a good idea to explain why you cannot allow him to continue the disturbances he is making and to ask him for suggestions of how he would like you to handle the problem if he does not change his actions.

Many times students know more about the reasons for their misbehavior than they realize. Often they have acceptable ideas of how to cope with it. If you say to a student, "John, you disrupt the entire class when you whistle. I've asked you to stop several times and you seem to do it anyway. What do you think we ought to do about it? Your classmates and I can't concentrate when you whistle. How can we handle the problem?" The student will frequently offer a clue such as "I read this book last term or these problems are too easy. I'm bored." He might say something as obvious as, "I forget that I'm in class and I don't even realize what I'm doing." His answer should tell you how to handle the problem. Give him another book to read or more difficult problems to work on or nod to remind him when he begins whistling. If his problem is one of constant talking to his neighbor, without blaming him or his friend, you might try changing his seat to another section of the room. If this doesn't work, you can take more drastic measures.

Conclude your interview by asking him how he thinks you should handle the problem the next time it arises. You will not change his seat a second time so more severe measures will be required. Sometimes the pupil will offer appropriate punishments for subsequent infractions. If so, tell him that you will follow his proposals. If not, offer your own alternatives so the student knows what he is to expect the next time he becomes a problem.

In many instances you will discover that pupils who misbehave in class are calling out for some personal attention. Your interest and willingness to consider their points of view and their problems may make allies for you out of potentially disruptive forces.

MAKE ALLOWANCES FOR INDIVIDUAL HANDICAPS

If a student is a discipline problem because he cannot concentrate on his work and does not keep up with the other students, check his records in the guidance and medical offices. These reports may provide information on optical, hearing and speech problems for which you could compensate by changing seats or adjusting assignments. Often, medical records will reveal speech difficulties which will account for a student's refusal to answer your questions or participate

36

in oral drills. Auditory weaknesses may explain a student's failure to answer you when you speak to him. The school nurse or doctor might also suggest ways in which you could be of help to the student.

A check on the academic records of a pupil might reveal that he is in your class as a result of a rostering error. If the work is too far above or below his capabilities he is bound to become disinterested and turn into a discipline problem. With the help of the counselors and school medical authorities, many adjustment problems can be dealt with without causing the student to endure more stress than is necessary.

BE AWARE OF STUDENTS' CAPABILITIES
AND ACHIEVEMENT LEVELS

Based on the results of the diagnostic tests you administered on the opening days of school and the standardized test results kept in the students' records, be certain that the work you are assigning is neither too far above nor below their capabilities. Presenting material which is not directed to the students' ability levels is the easiest way to lose the cooperation and attention of your class. When pupils turn their attention away from your lessons, they promptly direct it toward ways to get into trouble and to tempt their peers to join them. Arranging lessons which will meet the needs of individuals with differences in ability and interest will help to prevent problems from arising.

RELATE YOUR SUBJECT MATTER
TO IMMEDIATE NEEDS

The majority of secondary school pupils are incapable of striving for long-range goals. This is especially true in the lower grades and with slower students. You will never gain a student's cooperation by telling him that he must read *Lorna Doone* in the seventh grade so that he can get into college when he graduates in six years. It is not sufficiently motivating to tell students that they must learn the method for determining the area of a rectangle in case they ever try to build their own homes or that they should study French in case they win a free trip to France on a quiz program. You must devise ways, even resorting to games and puzzles if you have to, to make your subject immediately interesting. In order to be effective, you have to present your material in such a way that it is stimulating and relevant to their present needs. Students who do not see the relevancy or enjoyment in the lessons you are presenting are prime candidates for discipline problems. The materials for your students should be selected carefully so that you are certain that they are relevant to their immediate situations and experiences. While it is true that you will be given certain specific textbooks and curriculum guides which the school district and your department chairman will expect you to complete with your classes during the semester, it is your responsibility to find ways to make those materials relevant and meaningful to your pupils. Sometimes, this can be done most effectively if you combine your efforts with those of other subject-matter teachers to arouse pupil enthusiasm for learning. For example, a mathematics teacher and a biology teacher in Philadelphia worked with a social studies teacher to get their students interested in cleaning up a neighborhood eye-sore located adjacent to the schoolyard. The social studies teacher directed their letter-writing assignments to the proper local government officials who had the authority to grant permission for them to restructure the vacant lot into a small park-play area. The English teacher helped them to write letters to local merchants asking for needed supplies and to neighborhood newspapers to keep the community informed of their progress. The mathematics teacher helped the classes to determine what dimensions were needed for the play area and the foliage areas and how to place a path parallel to the longer sides of the park. The biology teacher taught them how to plant and care for the greenery which would flourish well in their locale. In the trade courses, the boys made signs directing people to stay off the grass, watch the flowers and be aware that the area had been improved by the students from the neighborhood junior high school. The pupils were motivated and enthusiastic because they saw practicality in what they were asked to learn.

Projects of this type involve a great deal of time, planning and cooperation on the part of the teachers involved. The results of increased learning, enthusiasm for learning and bolstered positive self-concepts of the classes involved make the return on the educators' time-investments more than worthwhile.

Few teachers have the time to become involved in projects as complex as the one just described. However, all educators can and should relate their subject matter to the personal lives and interests of their pupils. They must be willing to make the necessary effort and time-investment to do so. Mathematics teachers can use problems involving recipes and car mileage figures to explain the use of fractions. English teachers can relate popular music to literary themes and novel characters to television heroes. Social studies teachers can show the relationship between historical characters and movie heroes and between the organizations of street gangs and the offices and levels of government. These are only a few simple suggestions to give the novice an idea of the kinds of things which can be done in the classroom to stimulate learning. There are many other possibilities which will occur to the teacher once she is in her classroom interacting with her pupils.

While many of these suggestions may seem more like theatrical techniques than learning devices, the new teacher will soon realize that gaining her students' interest in learning is the major campaign of the educational war. No opportunity for stimulating the pupil's desire to learn, except those which are demeaning to the educator's dignity or dangerous to the pupils' physical or emotional security, should be overlooked.

DELEGATE RESPONSIBILITY

Delegating responsibility is a helpful technique in maintaining classroom control. Having students take care of time-consuming menial chores frees the teacher to focus her full attention on the class. Giving students duties to carry out can also be a means of gaining the cooperation and allegiance of troublesome pupils who threaten to become misbehavers. Small jobs can be invented and given to gain the allegiance of troublesome pupils. The boy who is constantly tugging on the window shades with the intention of disrupting the class when they roll up loudly can be assigned to see that the window shades are always even with one another. The girl who shuffles her feet restlessly near the end of the period can be asked to quietly wave her hand to signal the teacher five minutes before class time expires so that she can begin ending her lesson. The student who shreds papers and blows the confetti across the room should be designated to make certain the floors are clean before class is dismissed by reminding everyone to pick up their scraps and taking the basket around to collect the debris. The pupil who overturns movable chairs and desks whenever the opportunity presents itself can become the chief row-straightener.

The wise teacher can select many more jobs to fit her pupils' misbehavior patterns or nervous habits. It is vitally important to the effectiveness of this technique that the teacher propose these jobs to the students with sincerity. Class members should not be made to feel that they are being punished. There is time for punishment later if this technique is unsuccessful. The job should be offered to the student as though you are asking him to help you because you honestly need his help to make things easier for you in the classroom. If the student declines the position, there is nothing to be gained from trying to force him into accepting it or from threatening him with punishment. This would only increase his feelings of animosity. Later in the term he might be more receptive to the idea and you can approach him again at that time or try another method to reach him.

SET UP STANDARDS OF DEPORTMENT

Certain attainable standards of behavior must be established for every classroom as well as for the school as a whole. Many of these standards, while obvious to the teacher, must be reemphasized and enforced daily if the teacher expects the students to observe them. While you might feel foolish listing rules which seem to you as though they should be automatic practices, the standards you expect your classes to meet must be reviewed clearly at the beginning of the term and frequently thereafter to offset potential misbehavior.

You should demand that your pupils be in class on time at the beginning of each period unless they can present a written excuse from a reliable source such as another teacher or administrator. A note from another pupil, even a responsible pupil such as the editor of the school paper or a student council official, is not acceptable. If you don't enforce this rule, latecomers will disrupt other pupils as they noisily enter the room and brush past classmates who are already working. Once you allow pupils to come to class whenever they feel like it, you will have pupils stopping off for cigarettes, snacks, naps, card games and romantic interludes on the way to your room.

Students must be required to bring their books, writing implements and supplies to class daily. Some students will use the excuse that they cannot afford to purchase school supplies as an explanation for their unpreparedness. Do not accept this. Most schools have emergency funds available to cover just such situations. If such a fund is nonexistent, you can try to get the supplies from the school's reserves. If this is not feasible, it would be to your advantage to purchase the needed supplies for the pupil yourself and then require him to "work off the loan" by filing papers, straightening your book closet, carrying supplies to storage areas, and running errands for the office. The student should be made to feel that he must earn the supplies. Otherwise, he will have little respect for their value and will try to take advantage of your kindness in the future. Do not allow students to come without papers

41

and pencils. Students who are unprepared to participate in classwork will distract their peers to keep themselves amused. If you don't enforce rules of preparation, you will find that you have classes of bored, disruptive students or you will spend the first portion of your class time distributing reams of paper and boxes of pencils. Since it is usually most difficult to pry these items from the grasps of supply chairmen, they should not be distributed freely.

Although the idea of refusing to give pencils and paper to students sounds like pettiness to the novice, the experienced teacher will confirm the fact that once you establish this practice, your pupils will rarely bother to be prepared. Why carry things to class and try to keep track of them in the lunchroom if the teacher will give them to you once you arrive?

Try to remember that one of your functions as a teacher is to prepare your charges for what comes next. Next is usually a job, college, the service or marriage. An employer will not allow waitresses or mechanics to work without their uniforms. A college professor will not supply pencils and papers with his lectures. The drill sergeant will not allow a soldier to march without a clean rifle and a husband will expect his meals and clean shirts to be ready when he wants them and will not overlook their absence. Therefore, permitting unpreparedness is performing a great disservice to your pupils. While constant reminders consume valuable time in the beginning of the term, they will save you time and irritation once your classes are trained.

You must be certain, before requiring pupils to buy supplies other than the common ones such as pencils and paper, that your demands are reasonable. Don't, for example, ask your classes to purchase a six-dollar book for outside reading or a twenty-five dollar slide rule or a four-dollar drawing pencil. Requests such as these are unfair to the pupils and their parents.

In addition to demanding that your students be ready to work in your room, you must expect them to behave respectfully toward you and their peers. The class must remain quiet and attentive when you are speaking to them. Never try to talk over the conversations of pupils. It doesn't matter whether two people are speaking or the entire class is talking. You never begin to teach until everyone is silent. You are only lowering yourself in your own estimation and in that of your pupils if you attempt to speak above the din of other voices. You will present a pathetic and foolish figure if you virtually plead with your class for their attention while they make a mockery of your efforts.

When there is noise in the room, stand in front of the class and say nothing. Eventually they will realize that you are waiting for them to respond to you with silence. Even if you must stand at the front of the room for an entire class period without saying a word, you have made a point and the pupils have learned something. They have learned that if anything is to be accomplished, they must be quiet and that you will not teach while they are talking. Fortunately for the educator, there are always more students in the class who are concerned about grades and graduation than there are those who want only to have a good time. The former type of pupil will become bored with talking to his friends and will begin telling the others to keep quiet. The second class period you might only have to wait twenty minutes for your point to become clear and the following day your waiting time will decrease to ten minutes. Eventually they will settle down as soon as they see you waiting for them. Much more is accomplished by using the "standing in front of the room and waiting" technique than is achieved by yelling over their noise and pleading with them to settle down or by slamming books on your desk to startle them. Both of the latter methods only serve to add to the noise already prevalent in the room.

Difficult as it is to refrain from hollering, you should remember that when you are yelling, the students who are talking must raise their voices to be heard above your noise. When you stand before the class refusing to lower yourself to their childish behavioral patterns, you are maintaining your dignity and self-respect while accomplishing as much, if not more, than you would be by begging them to listen to you. The students know they are in the class to learn and after a short time will stop talking and begin trying to find out why no teaching is taking place. Try to remember that the odds are in your favor. Even the slowest and most reluctant students will balk at sitting in a classroom and doing nothing for long periods of time. Once these pupils stop talking, they will castigate the few who continue to cause disruptions. Then you can announce that you are ready to begin when there is total silence.

If you expect your students to respond favorably to your behavioral standards, you must extend to them the same courtesies you demand. Do not speak to another student or a visitor while a pupil is talking to you and his classmates. If a visitor enters the room to speak to you, ask him to wait at the door until your student is finished. If the intruder's business appears to be urgent, or the student is delivering a long speech, quietly and apologetically interrupt him and ask him to wait until you have taken care of the messenger.

Do not work at your desk, read or write on the board while your students are answering questions. If you expect their undivided attention, you must give them yours.

ESTABLISH STANDARD PROCEDURES

Students, especially the more immature and less intelligent ones, desperately need established classroom practices and procedures on which they can rely. Many new teachers believe that standardizing classroom activities stifles creativity. This is not true. There is room for creativity within any organized system. It cannot be emphasized too emphatically that meaningful learning does not occur in the midst of chaos.

Being organized means that supplies are kept together in one place so students know where to find them without asking you where they are every time they need them. It means that homework and test papers are always distributed and collected the same way. It also means that the class work schedule remains constant. If you establish Friday as your testing day and Wednesday as the day for group work, changing this program confuses and unsettles the slower and more immature students. Maintaining an established routine helps the teacher because if she trains her students to bring their textbooks three days a week and to be prepared for a test every Friday and to arrange the chairs at the beginning of the class for group work on still another day, she saves herself a lot of time and avoids explanations and having to cope with unprepared pupils. Most slower students find this sort of routine very comforting. Your class schedule is one of the few stable things in their lives on which they can count. Brighter and more mature students are able to adapt to schedule alterations more easily but still function at peak efficiency in a structured situation.

Adhering to a routine serves functions other than giving the pupils something to rely upon. It helps students who are absent to be prepared to participate in classwork on the day they return. A student returning on Wednesday knows from experience that he must bring his drill books because Wednesday is always the day for drill work and he knows that if he comes back on Thursday he should bring a current events article for the same reason.

This type of scheduling helps substitutes who take over in your absence. They will not have to cope with "Miss Jones never makes us do that" or "Mr. Smith just lets us talk on Thursday." Instead, they will have pupils who have the materials they need to do the lessons you left for them and who know what is expected of them.

You will also have to establish procedures for distributing and collecting books, papers and supplies. If you don't, you will not only lose many books, but will have students wandering around the room and up to your desk or closet to personally hand you their homework or return their books. With books, it is a good practice to have two permanent "bookboys" who get the texts from the closet and distribute the required number of books to the first person on each row. Then allow them to pass the books down or across the rows. Have them count out the books first so that they give the first person on each row only the exact number of books they need. The first person then takes a book for himself and passes the rest back or across the row to his classmates. The books should be collected in the same manner and the "bookboys" should count them before returning them to the closet. This avoids confusion and lost books.

Homework and test papers should be collected in a similar manner. They can be passed forward to the first person on each row and then collected across the front of the room. Another equally efficient way is to have them all passed to the row closest to the window or the door and then passed forward so that the first person in one row ends up with all of the papers. Then you can pick them up from him or her.

Standard forms should also be established for arranging homework and test papers. Requirements for neatness and uniformity are needed also. The reasons for this are more practical than aesthetic. If you don't require homework to be done in ink (with the possible exception of mathematics problems) on 8" by 11" paper with student names, the date and section or group numbers in a specified corner of the page, you will receive homework done on tablet paper, laundry wrappings, letter paper, sandwich bags and confetti-sized scraps. It will be written in multi-colored ink, crayon, lipstick and sometimes even in an unidentifiable substance strangely reminiscent of human blood. The beginning teacher has not really come into her own as an educator until she has tried to decipher an assignment written in four shades of felt pen which has been crumbled into a snowball-like form to such a degree that it must be ironed before it becomes remotely close to readable.

You must also emphasize that students are required to do the assignment in its entirety. You should not accept the three questions the student answered on the bus going home and the two he answered in the car coming back in the morning in place of the nine problems you assigned. Furthermore, penalties for lateness must be strictly enforced.

Be certain that none of your rules or procedures run contrary to established school policy. For example, many schools have specific testing days for the different subject areas. This is done to prevent students from having to take tests in four subjects on the same day. If the test day for your subject is Thursday, don't set Wednesday as the day for your examinations. It is unfair to the students and to your colleagues who will have to handle complaints from their classes.

You cannot prohibit practices in your classroom which school policy permits. If the school allows females to wear slacks to school, you cannot forbid them from entering your room if they are doing so. You might state that you prefer that they not wear slacks, but you cannot penalize them if they choose to do so when the school policy condones it. In the same manner, you cannot permit them to wear slacks in your room if school regulations forbid them to do so. Established school rules always take precedence over your own.

Try to remember at all times that in addition to teaching your specific subject matter, you are trying to prepare your pupils to function effectively in the business and social worlds. Even those who go on to college will never exist in an academic vacuum encompassed only by your subject matter. Employers and friends will not accept partially-completed work, carelessness, lateness or disrespect. Neither should you.

NEVER THREATEN OR CHALLENGE A STUDENT

People will go to any lengths to defend their egos. This is especially true in the case of adolescents. If a teacher tells a student he "wouldn't dare" do something, he must do it in order to protect his friends' opinions of him as well as his own self-image. For the same reason, never reprimand, castigate or tease a student in front of his peers. In order to defend his standing with his classmates, he will be forced to lash out at you.

When a student misbehaves in class, it is a good policy to ask him to speak to you after class without commenting on his infractions. Even if he tries to prod you into an argument or confrontation, calmly tell him that you don't intend to take class time to discuss it. Promise to speak with him about it at length when the period ends. The chances of your getting an apology, a promise of better behavior, or at least arriving at a compromise with the student are far greater when the matter is being handled privately than when you are before an audience of his friends.

Never threaten to take action against a student unless you are certain that you can take the steps you promised legally, morally and within the framework of the school rules. If you promise to have a student expelled from school for chewing gum and throwing paper airplanes while you are trying to teach and the school administration refuses to support your demands for his expulsion, you have seriously undermined your position with the student and with the class because they will see that the troublemaker is still in the room and that you have a very red face. If you threaten to take a course of action against a student when he confronts you, you must be prepared to take whatever action you indicated. Otherwise, your promises and threats will be very much open to suspicion. You will lose both your students' respect and their trust.

DON'T RAISE YOUR VOICE UNNECESSARILY

As previously explained, raising your voice when you are trying to quiet your class or gain its attention, only adds to the uproar. The vicious cycle of your voice being raised above theirs, and theirs being raised above yours, continues until the din can be heard several corridors away.

A much wiser practice is to speak softly. Your voice should be just above a whisper. The pupils will become curious and will lower their voices or stop their conversations entirely to hear what you are saying. Eventually the room will become quiet enough for you to be heard without hollering and, in an even tone, you can ask your pupils for their total attention and silence.

DO NOT COMMIT INFRACTIONS OF THE RULES

Never do those things which you or school policy will not permit the students to do. If students are not permitted to smoke in the school or on the school grounds, it is very difficult to explain why you come out of the teachers' lounge smelling of smoke. If the school has a dress code to which it requires pupils to adhere, you should be certain that your personal attire and appearance conform to regulations. Students will not accept the idea that they cannot wear very short or very long skirts when their teachers do or that their male teachers wear long hair and beards when they must be closely-cropped and clean shaven.

NEVER INFLICT UNIVERSAL PUNISHMENT

Surveys have indicated that students emphasize the importance of a teacher's fairness above most other personal qualities. There are few practices which are quite as unjust as punishing the innocent along with the guilty. Never punish an entire class for the infractions of a few. Aside from the obvious fact that it is not fair, it is one of the easiest ways to give rise to class resentment. It would be more to your advantage to ignore an incident if you are unable to identify the troublemakers than to alienate the well-behaved students by inflicting punishment on them that they don't deserve. Castigating innocent pupils is a certain means of turning them into difficult students. The logic behind this is very understandable. If they're going to be punished for things they haven't done, shouldn't they enjoy the fun that goes with breaking the rules?

AVOID SARCASM

All secondary school students greatly resent sarcasm. Teachers who resort to giving sarcastic answers are evidencing insecurity and are inviting sarcastic replies from resentful and unruly pupils. Such word exchanges invite disruptive situations to occur. They encourage a student to make disrespectful remarks to the teacher who then must castigate him for being fresh. To regain his self-respect, he must reply to the teacher and a verbal war ensues. Such confrontations in which neither the teacher nor pupil want to back down are easily prevented if sarcasm is avoided.

CHECK YOUR PERSONAL MANNERISMS

When you are before the class, try to avoid all nervous mannerisms which might distract and amuse the class. Many teachers unconsciously pace back and forth while they are talking, rub a piece of chalk between their hands, twirl a key chain or tug on their clothes. After a short time, students begin keeping track of the number of times the teacher touches her belt or pulls on her ear. They listen to hear her clear her throat more raptly than they heed her words of wisdom.

The nervous mannerisms a teacher displays invite pupils to mimic her behind her back or to her face which is often worse and considerably more damaging to the educator's ego and self-confidence. Occasionally, if the teacher is truly unpopular, the pupils might draw pictures on the board or taunt her about her habits to embarrass her and make her feel uncomfortable.

Concentrate on your voice control. Be certain that you speak loud enough to be heard in the rear of the room without being loud enough to be heard in the next classroom. Avoid wide ranges in pitch. Try to keep your voice from cracking, screeching or droning. If you are aware that you have a problem with voice control, in addition to making a conscious effort to overcome your problems, you might ask the school's speech therapist for suggestions to help you speak effectively.

Try to make variations in your dress patterns. Do not wear the same colors to school daily. Try to rotate your clothes so that you do not wear the same dress or suit to class two days in a row. Teen-agers are very concerned with fashions and current styles. They are very critical of dress patterns, hair styles, and the amount and kind of make-up their female teachers wear. Select hair and clothing styles which are fashionable but not extreme. Extremes in personal appearance draw your students' attention away from your lessons and hinder the learning process. They will also give students something to mock in the unflattering caricatures they so often feel impelled to draw of teachers during your lessons.

Do not isolate favorite pupils. An educator cannot help but favor the sweet little girl who raises her hand to answer every question correctly or the boy who falls over his feet in an attempt to open the door or carry books for his instructor. The educator must be very careful not to allow her personal preferences to become obvious. Every teacher is attracted to students who remind them of themselves when they were young or who look like their children or kid brothers and sisters. However, students are very perceptive and will be resentful of both you and the pupils you have chosen to favor. They will invent devious ways to torture the favored pupils and will feel less kindly toward you. Everything that can be done to make you and their preferred peers miserable will be tried. Simply because they are in the majority, they are more than likely to annoy you and succeed in taunting their classmates to the limit of their endurance.

Maintaining classroom control is vitally important if the educational process is to take place. It is important not only in the individual classroom but also in relationship to the functioning of the entire school. Noise from your room invades other classrooms making it difficult for the teacher

51

there to teach her lesson and control her class. It makes it impossible for students in nearby rooms to concentrate on their lessons. The noise from your room filters into administrative offices and distracts officials and secretaries. It also shows your supervisors that you are having difficulty directing your class and this will tend to result in uninvited visitors inspecting your domain more frequently than is usually required.

Students who leave your room in an unruly fashion continue their rowdy behavior at their next stop. They enter their next teacher's classroom in an excited state and she has to calm them down before attempting to teach them. They torture bus drivers and frighten the members of the neighboring community with boisterous behavior in the streets if they leave the school directly from your classroom. Besides being a reflection of your inadequacy as an educator, turning rowdy students loose on unsuspecting professionals and laymen is very unfair.

Tolerating lack of control and organization in your classroom affects your self-respect because students notoriously push you and test you as far as they can to see how much they can get away with. Difficult as it is for a new teacher who is going through the "test of fire" to believe, the students actually want you to emerge victorious. They know that unless they break you down completely and send you in tears to join a convent or the foreign legion, they will have to put up with you for the entire semester. They would prefer, for obvious reasons, to have a teacher they can like and respect. Even the most difficult pupils tire of "taunt the teacher" games after a few weeks and would rather have a "good guy" before them every day than a mass of quivering flesh and rattling bones.

Loss of control undermines your position with your colleagues and superiors and defeats the entire purpose of education, to say nothing of what student persecution and humiliation can do to your ego. The once-victorious student oppressors will find increasingly more devastating ways to blast away at your self-respect. All of your good intentions, college degrees and honors will not comfort you at night when students throw oranges and shout obscenities at you during the day. Therefore, it is vitally important for you, your students and the welfare of the entire school that you make every effort to offset trouble before it begins by remaining in total control of your classroom at all times.

Chapter Four

Discipline

Discipline and punishment are very delicate matters for the educator to handle. Although it is generally accepted that the teacher functions "in loco parentis," in place of the parent, she does not have all the rights and privileges granted to the parent. There are only certain punitive measures the teacher is permitted to take without encountering serious repercussions. She cannot, for example, slap a student across the face when he makes an insolent remark. Because of the limitations placed upon the educator's punitive authority, it is wise for her to do everything she possibly can to avoid situations requiring her to administer punishment or take disciplinary action. However, no matter how organized, calm, experienced and concerned a teacher is, there will still be times in every school term when she will have to exchange the role of the educator for that of the disciplinarian.

Situations requiring the punishment of students usually arise spontaneously. Teachers do not enter the classroom each period expecting to discipline pupils. When these situations do arise, teachers, being only human, experience the natural emotion of anger combined with a tinge of fear that authority and dignity will not remain triumphant at the end of the confrontation. Novices combine these natural feelings with large portions of panic. When grouped together, these sentiments often encourage the teacher to make wild threats she later finds she cannot carry out, or to commit acts she wishes she could retract. Such confrontations only serve to undermine the teacher's self-respect and shake her credibility and self-confidence. Positive steps should be taken to prevent these things from happening.

Before situations requiring disciplinary action occur, the teacher should discover what recourses are available to her should she ever need them. She should check to be certain that any action she wants to take is not against school rules. She must also determine that anything she wishes to do is not detrimental to the child's physical, intellectual or emotional development. Preventing a child from attending a class he enjoys, taking away his lunch period or humiliating him in front of his peers are all types of punishment which will cause more repercussions for the teacher than for the punished student.

Most schools have established policies for dealing with infractions of school rules. Therefore, check with administrators or more experienced teachers to determine what these regulations are. For example, many schools have set procedures for dealing with chronic class-cutters, smokers, and hallway lingerers. Find out what these policies are before you threaten to take any action. Also, try to determine how strictly these rules and policies are adhered to. You would not want to be the only teacher strictly enforcing a fifty-year-old rule that most teachers and students have long since forgotten. It is very embarrassing to punish a student and then find that you have to retract your punishment because it is contrary to the established school policy or because it runs contrary to the student's well-being.

Many acceptable types of punishment will present themselves to you within the framework of the school situation. The most obvious and widely-used forms of punishment are keeping students after school and removing privileges, such as not allowing them to attend or participate in extra-curricular activities. If you keep a student after school, use that time wisely. Don't allow students to sit idly for an hour staring out of the window or shredding paper. Many discipline problems are also scholastic problems. Use the time after school to review his work or suggest outside work he can do if he is a superior student. Some discipline problems are the result of personal difficulties which might be solved in a private discussion. When you do have to keep a pupil after school, remember that it is wise never to detain a student of the opposite sex after school unless you have another student present. Always try to keep another student after school even if it is on the pretext of straightening the book closet or reviewing a test paper. If this is not possible, do not conduct your after-school meeting with a single pupil in your classroom. Move to a more highly-populated area such as a bench in the counseling office or the department head's office. Students who feel they have been unjustly punished are prone to make many unfounded charges which could ruin a teacher's reputation, if not her entire career, even after it has been proven that there is no substance to the charge.

In selecting disciplinary techniques never use schoolwork to punish a pupil. Do not assign extra homework or drills to punish a student. He should not have to copy pages from his literature book or be told "Because you were talkative in class you have to do fifteen extra mathematics problems." The reason for this is obvious. If you want pupils to have a positive reaction toward your subject matter, you should never use it in a negative situation.

When you plan your disciplinary measures, it is important that the quantity of the punishment fit the crime. If you punish students severely for talking while you are trying to teach or for arriving at class late, what more extreme degree of punishment are you going to hand out for carrying a knife or beating another student? Therefore, it is important that you do not let your anger over being disobeyed or ignored goad you into inflicting an unreasonable amount of punishment.

One method of assigning a suitable punishment is to try to have the students correct or repair any damage they might have done. The students who carve words in the wooden desk tops can be required to sand them down and refinish them after school or during recreation periods. The students who destroy books and materials can be put to work in the book closets or supply rooms of the school until they "work off" the cost of the materials. Pupils who mutilate decorations should replace them during their free time.

Often, when pupils are told to come after school to repair damage or sit out a detention, they rely on the excuse that they can't come because their family's economic situation requires them to take a job after school or to care for younger sisters and brothers while their parents work. If you can determine that their excuse is valid by talking directly to parents, knowledgeable guidance personnel or colleagues, arrange for the pupils to come before school or during a portion of their lunch periods. Notice I said a portion of the lunch period. A teacher who denies a student sufficient time to obtain nourishment is inviting trouble for herself. Such an act is universally frowned upon even though students frequently eat during your class period and save their lunch periods for social activities.

It is best for discipline to be handled by the classroom teacher herself without involving outside help. Students who see teachers running to authorities for help in handling situations they should have been able to cope with themselves realize they have an incompetent or frightened person before them. They will use this awareness to its fullest advantage and persecute the teacher unmercifully. Students who are sweet, charming, kind and angelic individually become mean, cruel, rotten and nasty when they join forces to show their collective superiority over a teacher who has shown that she cannot stand up to their shows of strength. They hum, whistle, stomp feet, eat lunches, giggle, crack chewing gum, tickle neighbors and do any other annoying things which they know will make an adult who goes to the principal for help in handling them seem very foolish and immature. Imagine how your prestige with your principal will decline when you tell him you can't control your class because girls giggle and

58

the boys tap their pencils on the desks. To a man who has just tried to stop a gang confrontation in the boys' locker room, your problems will seem inconsequential and indicative of incompetence. Once a teacher has admitted to an inability to control her classes, her superiors are always on the lookout for signs of trouble. The teacher's classroom freedom is undermined. Ignoring these little games will stop them faster than pleading, screaming or crying. The students are trying to rattle and confuse you. If they are not successful with their minor torture techniques, they will abandon them. If you have handled yourself in a dignified manner which does not reek of over-confidence, they will turn their thoughts toward your lessons and save their antics for someone less able to stand up to the strain.

The best approach for handling individual discipline problems, such as those involving insubordination, is to first separate the troublemaker from the rest of the class. The days of the public pillory have long since passed. If you attempt to discipline an unruly pupil in the presence of his classmates, he is going to rebel by going to greater extremes than his original infringement in an attempt to protect his self-respect and class standing. Therefore, if a pupil is disrespectful to you in class, rather than arguing about his misbehavior with him in front of the class, quietly tell him to see you after class to discuss the problem. This gives him the entire class period to worry about what you are going to do. His classmates wonder also. Even though he talks to his classmates after your meeting and tells them how he triumphed over you during your confrontation, they can never be sure who emerged the victor. Never lower yourself to engaging in verbal fisticuffs before a class. You are most certain to emerge as the loser since you are in the minority.

Schools have strict rules about objects which are not to be brought to school. Knives, guns, pipes and sticks are the most obvious ones. Other schools forbid transistor radios from being brought into the building. When you discover a student with a possession he should not have you should, of course, try to separate him from it. Do not attempt to do this by force, however. Nothing looks sillier than a teacher who has lost her footing while trying to grab a dirty magazine away from a student and who ends up sprawled all over a desk. Simply ask the pupil to give you the forbidden item. If he refuses, ask him to see you after class and again request that he give it to you. If the object is not illegal like a gun or knife, and if it is something which cannot be inexpensively replaced, such as a radio, it should be returned to the pupil from whom it was taken, at the end of the school day. Do not return it to him at the end of your period so that he can plague a fellow teacher with music seeping from a hidden spot in the back of the room. If the object is one which is potentially harmful or illegal, you should turn it in to the principal or disciplinary officer who will be acquainted with the procedures for confiscating such material. If the student refuses to give you the gun or knife, don't try to take it by force. Allow him to leave but immediately report the student and the object to your superiors who will then take appropriate measures to alert security personnel to apprehend the pupil.

A class lesson should not be interrupted to handle minor discipline problems such as chronic talking, turning around or inattention. Should any of these annoying, but minor disruptions occur, the teacher would be wise to discreetly walk toward the seat of the misbehaver and tap him on the shoulder, stare at him from the front of the room, or point to him until a neighbor nudges him. All of these can be done without interrupting the continuity of your lesson.

Some students are chronic latecomers to class. They interrupt the class when they enter the room because they distract their classmates from their studies. For this reason alone it is wise to stop all lateness. Another obvious reason is to teach the student that he must be punctual for your class just as he will have to be for a job. Requiring the pupils to "repay" missed minutes at the beginning of their lunch periods when they are anxious to be first in food lines or at the end of the day when they are anxious to board busses early will help to prevent this problem.

Although it is best for the teacher to handle as much of the discipline of her class as she possibly can, there are certain cases in which she must ask for outside assistance or at least make administrative authorities aware of the misbehavior which has occurred in her room. She should also inform them of what action she has taken. In cases in which illegal activities have occurred, where she or other students have been physically abused or threatened, or where the teacher is outnumbered or is physically incapable of handling a disturbance, help must be called for. In all cases, the teacher must protect the physical well-being of her pupils. Students who are discovered carrying weapons, who threaten fellow students and teachers, who steal or try to steal materials belonging to others, set fires, or who threaten physical harm to others should be reported to the principal or disciplinarian who will then decide if the infraction should be reported to law enforcement officials.

If students do not comply with the punishment you inflict, do not report for detentions or make restitution of materials they have destroyed, this too should be reported to higher authorities. But first you must make every effort to handle the situation yourself.

Should trouble arise in the classroom which you are incapable of handling, such as a class becoming totally unruly and abusive, send a reliable student for help. This is especially true of female teachers who need the assistance of strong men. Male students in the upper grades of senior high schools are very big and very strong. Occasionally, they become uncontrollable, especially if you are a 90-pound five-foot tall female novice. The intelligent female can sometimes use her size to her advantage by appealing to their protective male instincts. However, if this does not prove to be successful and the class becomes uncontrollable, the teacher should send a reliable student for help. Direct him to go to the principal, disciplinary head or the first big male

61

teacher he meets in the hallway. In those schools located in very troublesome areas, your only reliable students are often those who are smaller than their peers or who are defenseless females. It might be wise in such situations to send your messengers in pairs of twos. You should never leave the classroom yourself or permit the students to be without adult supervision. If you do, you are responsible for injuries or property damage which occurs in your absence.

At times, particularly in the upper grades, you might find students acting irrationally in class. If you have even the slightest suspicion that the student is under the influence of drugs or alcohol, send one student to obtain administrative help while another goes to the medical division for assistance. Such pupils represent potential danger to themselves as well as to their peers. The school nurse and principal have more experience in dealing with drug and alcohol users than you have and will know what action to take both medically and legally. While waiting for help to arrive, try to take precautions against the student's harming himself or his classmates.

Should a fight break out between two or more of your students, don't try to step between them to try to break up the altercation. The chances are that if you do, you will receive most of the blows. When a fight begins, get two or more of your stronger students to hold each of the fighters. Send the participants to separate corners of the room. You can begin mediation or file reports with the administration after class is over. Do not wait to secure medical attention, however. Any bleeding should be stopped immediately and broken bones should be set by the school physician without delay.

When you select disciplinary actions for your students be careful that you do not punish an entire class for the infractions of a few. Case studies have revealed that pupils consider a teacher's fairness more important than her knowledge of her subject matter. There is nothing quite as unfair as punishing innocent people for the crimes of the guilty.

If you cannot determine who the actual troublemakers are in a given situation, it is often to your advantage to disregard the entire matter rather than castigating an entire class.

Another way of handling group misbehavior is to calmly discuss the consequences of the act while not pointing an accusing finger at anyone. Such a discussion might sound something like: "I know that only a few of you participated in drawing slogans and pictures all over the walls, but I hope that those of you who were responsible will not do it again. It is not very funny and I'm certain those of you involved now realize how childish it was. Now we'll have to stay after school to wash the walls. It means double the amount of wasted work—work for those who wrote the slogans and work for those who must erase them. In the future let's all save the work and not write on the walls. If you feel you must draw pictures, speak to me first and I'll try to get some art supplies for you."

Sometimes it is to the teacher's benefit to overlook minor episodes of misbehavior or to be selectively deaf, blind and dumb. If a teacher overhears something she wasn't supposed to, such as a derogatory remark made about her by one of her students, or an obscene utterance by one pupil to another, she would be better off ignoring the remark if she possibly can than forcing the pupil to repeat it or making an issue out of it. Students, especially those in the lower grades, drop their books on cue at a predetermined time or sneeze simultaneously. Then they break into gales of hysterical laughter. More time will be lost if you burst into tirades of angry words than if you ignore the entire incident. If you show no reaction at all, they will be more discouraged than if you punish them.

In your relationships with your pupils, be yourself. If a student in the back of the room feels impelled occasionally to say something which the class finds terribly funny, and you think it's funny, join in the laughter, and then get back to the business at hand. Don't try to be stern in a harmless situation which you and your pupils can enjoy together.

Your pupils' parents can prove to be invaluable in helping you to discipline them. When a problem first arises you might call the parents and sincerely ask them for their help in dealing with whatever problem behavior their child has been exhibiting. It is extremely important that your tone be one which exhibits a sincere request for help rather than one which accuses the parents of failing to raise their child properly. Telling the parents about the problems you have been having and asking for their advice on how to handle the problem and reach the child will bring the school and home closer together. Both can then cooperate to give the student the optimum assistance in meeting his adjustment problems. This technique will also prevent parents from accusing the school of failing to notify them about their child's misbehavior. Often, the punishments the parents inflict are more severe and have a greater and more lasting effect upon the pupil than any means you might have used. Parents appreciate this personalized effort on your part more than most novices realize. The important part of this procedure is to remember to approach the parent with a manner which reflects your sincere desire to work with them to meet their child's individual needs. If, after speaking to the parents, you discover that they are not interested in their child's behavioral patterns or are not willing to cooperate with you, you can then proceed as though you had never contacted them and nothing has been lost.

If discipline is administered wisely and fairly by the classroom teacher, it can, in many instances, help to cement a good relationship between students and educator. Many ghetto-dwelling students come from home situations which are so poorly structured that the pupils desperately need someone to take the time to illustrate an interest in their behavior. The teacher who ignores a pupil's misbehavior or pushes the disciplining chores off onto another party is not only undermining her own authority and self-respect and backing down in the face of adversity, but she is also failing to fulfill the needs of her pupils who, in essence, are asking her to respond to their actions. She is behaving much like the parent who fails to discipline her child because she is disinterested or because she wants to buy her child's love by acquiescing to his every whim. Showing a definite interest in molding positive behavioral patterns is one way for a teacher to illustrate her dedication to her pupils. As teachers, we should be preparing our students to function effectively in the world outside the classroom. In addition to teaching them to use skills necessary to be self-supporting, we should also be molding them to be good citizens. To accomplish the latter, we must teach them to conform to acceptable standards of behavior, to respect the needs of others, and to expect to receive the consequences of their own actions. We owe this to the pupils, their parents, and the communities which employ us to protect their interests by developing useful, respectable citizens.

Chapter Five

Effective Lesson Planning

Effective lesson planning is one of the most vital segments of the educator's duties. Lessons must be planned and
organized in a manner which will enable the students to
understand and use the materials you are presenting. In
addition to structuring subject matter content into a compre-
hendible form, the successful teacher must make provisions
for motivating the pupils to want to learn the facts and skills
contained in the lessons. Pupil-motivation is one of the largest
campaigns of the educational battle. Preparing the motivational activities and planning the actual learning exercises
which follow are among the teacher's most important classroom functions. Fortunately, unlike the spontaneous discipline problems which arise frequently in the course of a normal
school day, the educator can prepare lesson plans well in
advance of the time they are to be used. This enables her
to make calm, conscientious decisions about what to include,
how to present the material and what provisions to make
for handling any possible unexpected occurrences such as
unusually high rates of absenteeism or shortages of books and
supplies.

The organization and presentation of meaningful lessons
is extremely important for two reasons. The most obvious
reason for teaching organized lessons is to insure the occurrence of effective learning. Many college graduates can recall
sitting in lecture halls listening to brilliant professors who
rambled on about dates, issues and people who, at the time,

seemed to be totally unrelated to each other and to the students. This type of experience is very frustrating at any level in the educational hierarchy, but it is especially disturbing for the immature secondary school minds which are incapable of collating concepts which are not presented to them directly and simply.

A secondary benefit gained from efficient lesson planning is that of making the teacher's job less complicated and more pleasant as a result of the increased class cooperation she receives from interested and receptive students. High levels of student enthusiasm offset the necessity for repetition, extra assistance in comprehension and the administration of discipline.

Each school system or district has an established set of basic objectives which must be fulfilled in each subject area within the course of the school year. In organizing the term's activities, the teacher must make provisions for meeting all of those requirements within the framework of her lesson plans because if she does not, her pupils will not be ready to do the assigned work at the next grade level. In addition, if the class does not cover all of the suggested skills, it will not be prepared to pass any final examinations which are administered on a schoolwide or citywide basis. Both of these consequences are unfair to the children and reflect poorly on the teacher's capabilities as an educator and a planner. Not covering all of the required work with your classes is also unfair to your fellow teachers. It makes planning difficult for those who will try to begin presenting material to your groups at anticipated levels of competence during the next semesters. Because students are placed in different classrooms at the end of each term as a result of scheduling expediencies, your colleagues will be forced to handle unnecessary differences in ability and experience if you do not cover all of your assigned work.

The classroom teacher is not free to make changes in curriculum materials or requirements simply because she personally does not like them. She is justified in making limited alterations within the boundaries of the curriculum guides to suit her individual preferences and to meet the needs of her pupils. However, to bring about broad changes in subject matter content and approach, she should volunteer to be a member of the curriculum or textbook committees. If this course of action is not feasible for a new staff member, the dissatisfied teacher should attend meetings of these groups to make her suggestions and opinions known to her peers. She can also have her ideas considered by speaking to those committee members she knows personally and by offering her suggestions to them. Although this is a longer way of accomplishing your ends, it is more advisable to go through the established channels for curriculum change than making unilateral alterations. Changing the curriculum on your own only serves to interrupt the continuity of your students' training and alienates you from those of your peers who worked hard to develop the original guides you were supposed to follow.

As a new teacher you would do well to rely upon the wisdom and experience of those more seasoned educators who devised the curriculum guidelines to which your school system requires you to adhere. Actually working in the classroom for several months will often show you that the new techniques and approaches you learned in college courses are not quite as practical in the classroom as you thought they'd be. In your first year of teaching, it would be wise for you to learn how to prepare a good, clear lesson and how to direct an efficient, smooth-working classroom. You have plenty of time to become a curriculum innovator in your second year.

Dividing the entire year's course work into weekly and monthly units and then subdividing the units into daily lesson plans is a difficult task. The problem is greater for English, social science, and language teachers than it is for science and mathematics teachers. In mathematics and science, teachers usually are able to follow the simple and obvious procedure of building complex skills upon elementary ones. English, foreign language and social studies teachers have to decide between two different approaches to lesson planning. Long-range lesson plans can follow one of two organizational patterns. The first is the unit plan and the second is the daily alternation plan.

The first type of lesson plan involves concentrating on one subject area until the study of the subject has been completed in its entirety. For example, an English class would read and discuss *Hamlet* every day until the play was thoroughly studied. Then the teacher would spend several weeks discussing grammar and composition. After completing that unit, she might spend several weeks on speech techniques and then proceed to a unit on word usage and spelling. A language teacher might begin the term's work with a unit on the people and customs of Spain. Then she would progress to Spanish grammar. Several weeks might be spent on pronunciation and then concentration would be directed toward Spanish literature before going on to study Spanish history. A few weeks later she might work with vocabulary drills and return to grammar for more advanced work. A social science teacher might concentrate on current events for a few weeks and then go on to a study of foreign relations, historical problems and finally to local civic problems. There is, in this type of approach, the opportunity for the integration of related skills in each unit, but the concentration remains fixed upon one specific subject area for a prolonged period of time.

In the daily alternation approach, the teacher divides the skills to be learned into different sections and scatters them throughout the week. The plan for an English classroom might look like this:

Monday: Composition
Tuesday: Spelling and word study
Wednesday: Grammar and usage
Thursday: Literature
Friday: Testing and Literature

In a social studies class the organizational plan could take the following form:

Monday: Current events
Tuesday: History
Wednesday: Foreign relations
Thursday: Local government
Friday: Testing and Debates

And in a foreign language course the schedule might look like this:

Monday: Vocabulary
Tuesday: Literature
Wednesday: History
Thursday: Grammar
Friday: Testing and Pronunciation

Notice that Friday always seems to come up as a testing day. One of the reasons that many teachers select this day for administering examinations is that Friday is the day on which most pupils seem to be very restless. When they are listless and inattentive it is a good idea to try to engage them in quiet work activities which require their undivided attention as opposed to attempting to conduct oral drills which permit two thirds of the class to concentrate on looking out of the windows while a few students are answering your questions. The only drawback to scheduling Friday as your test day is that if all the teachers do this students will be unfairly burdened. To avoid this, many schools assign specific test days to each individual subject so that no student will have to take more than one or two examinations on any given day. It would be wise, when planning your lessons, to see if your school follows such a system and do your best to conform to it.

This alternating type of scheduling is especially good for teaching slower learners and younger students whose attention spans are comparatively short. They tend to lose interest in activities which continue for more than one or two suc-

71

cessive class periods. However, this type of pupil desperately needs an organized plan upon which he can rely. They find security in knowing that every Thursday they are going to read a story and will have to bring their literature books to class. If they come to class on Wednesday and find that they are not going to work in their grammar books, they often become confused and angry. They are more apt to be prepared and participate in class work if such a specified plan is followed and if they are trained to have certain books and materials with them on definite days. This makes things easier for them and for the teacher.

Although following a definite daily plan sounds overly regulating and contrary to spontaneous creativity on the part of teachers and students, such is definitely not the case. The good teacher must always be flexible enough to deviate from her plans on those occasions when a class shows a decided interest in continuing an activity into the next class period. If a class becomes very enthusiastic about a piece of literature or a composition assignment, it should not be forced to wait an entire week to finish it because the over-all plan says the next day is designated as a grammar day. Common sense should indicate that whenever a class becomes interested in a learning experience, that experience should be continued until the children have gleaned all that they possibly can from it.

Both the alternating and the unit methods of organization can provide profitable learning experiences. Your decision about which method to follow should be based upon your judgment of your students' ability to concentrate on one subject area for a prolonged period of time, your own interest in discussing a subject at length and upon the availability of textbooks and supplies you need for your lessons. Many schools are plagued by textbook shortages which require the sharing of books and supplies by several classes. When you find yourself in this situation, you must alter your plans to accommodate the book schedules prepared by the department.

Once you have decided on the over-all approach you are going to take in presenting the semester's work, you have to separate the material into daily lesson plans. In so doing, it is a good practice to try to plan more activities than you expect to cover in a single period. If you do not discuss all the work you intended to, you can always resume the discussion on subsequent days. Over-planning is important because you will find that there is little that is quite as uncomfortable for you as a teacher as having fifteen minutes remaining in a period and forty students staring at you while you try to bluff through something that will hold their attention. Most students are perceptive enough to realize that you are stalling and that the material you are presenting is really inconsequential or irrelevant. If chaos doesn't result while you are talking about unimportant or repetitious subjects, you are at least certain to have boredom reigning in the classroom, which isn't any more desirable as an alternative.

While there is some choice available in the approach you decide to take in organizing the term's material, the pattern you should follow for preparing the daily class lessons is a rather set one. This basic lesson plan form has proven to be effective for lessons in all subject areas. There are seven distinct segments which should be provided for in planning all of your daily lessons. The novice should actually write out all seven parts for each lesson she plans to teach every day. This should be done at least one week in advance of the time you intend to present the lesson. Then, the night before, you can briefly review your lessons for the following day.

PRECLASS WORK

Preclass work serves both practical and educational functions. It is impossible to expect that all of your students will ever arrive at your classroom and be prepared to begin work simultaneously. Therefore, from the time the previous period ends until your actual classwork can begin, a time period of about eight minutes elapses and forty students enter the room. Those pupils who are coming from a few doors away will enter first and begin talking with each other while finding various ways to get into trouble or become rowdy and destructive. Some of them will have ample time to work themselves up into heated arguments over who pushed whom first at the pencil sharpener before all of their classmates have even entered the room. Once the entire class has arrived and is seated, you have minor chores to perform such as roll taking and distributing materials which will prevent you from beginning instruction immediately. Keeping the pupils from pinching, shoving, biting, stabbing, robbing, tickling, cursing, kissing and/or tripping you and each other while you are performing these tasks is a very difficult job. It is at this time that preclass work becomes functional.

Writing brief drills on the board or leaving rex-o-graphed sheets on a desk where pupils can pick them up as they enter the room are good procedures to follow for administering preclass work. You should begin giving this type of work early in the semester so that the students become accustomed to the routine of doing this work as a matter of habit as soon as they enter the room. The exercises should take no longer than five or six minutes to complete and should be reviewed orally in less than two or three minutes. Do not take the time to wait for stragglers to complete the work because you will be defeating your own purposes in giving the preclass work in the first place. If you wait for latecomers to finish their exercises, other students won't be motivated to begin working as soon as they enter the room.

Educationally, preclass work should be used to reenforce or review previous learning experiences, to introduce new concepts or to motivate the students' interest in new ideas you intend to present. The kind of activities you devise will depend upon your subject matter, but they should involve simple skills such as unscrambling terms relevant to the subject matter, rearranging words in a paragraph or sentence, filling in missing words, numbers, symbols or diagrams, matching columns of words and definitions, short problems and answers, thinking of examples to illustrate a rule or skill, or any other short drills which you can think of to give students the opportunity to use your subject matter.

In addition to reviewing the exercises orally in class before each new lesson actually begins, you can instruct students to keep the completed work in a section of their notebooks which you can check periodically to see if they are actually being done. Grading the work would defeat its purpose of providing a pleasant educational diversion for students while they are waiting for you to begin class activities. If the work is presented as a challenge or as a game, you are more likely to get your pupils to cooperate in doing their exercises than if you assign the drills as a job or task which must be completed and then graded.

AIM OR PURPOSE OF THE LESSON

For each lesson you teach you should have a clear purpose or aim in mind. Knowing why you want the children to learn the skill you are presenting will make it easier for you to show them why they should want to learn the material you are discussing.

It is a good idea to write the aim of the lesson on the board so that the students know what you expect them to achieve during the class period. You and the pupils can refer to the aim frequently throughout the lesson to see if they are achieving the goals established at the beginning of the period. Seeing the aim of the lesson posted on the board is impressive as well as helpful for classroom visitors such as your department head or school principal.

MOTIVATION

Every lesson should be preceded by some motivational activity. Once your students "turn you off" or "tune you out," as they can very easily do, it is difficult to regain their attention and participation. Therefore, you must do something at the beginning of the lesson to make them want to hear and learn what you have to say. If simply emphasizing the importance of the work and illustrating the relevancy of the skills you want them to master is not sufficient to gain their cooperation, you must resort to games, puzzles, tricks, stories and anything else you can think of to arouse their interest in your lesson. No matter how well-organized your lesson is or how stimulating your subject matter is, it is of no value if you can't get your pupils to listen to what you have to say.

METHODS AND ACTIVITIES

Many college students come out of college believing that the only way to convey ideas or teach skills is through the use of the lecture method. This is not true. In fact, such a one-sided approach will prove quite harmful. Most secondary school students do not have the attention or interest spans which are necessary to enable them to concentrate on a single activity or approach for an entire period. For this reason, it is a good idea to try to vary the methods and activities which are used during each class session.

The following is a list of techniques which can be used to supplement the straight lecture approach to conveying information:

1. Demonstrations — These are particularly helpful in science, music and art classes when the teacher illustrates an experiment or an artistic or musical form she wishes the students to emulate.

2. Written and oral drills — After a teacher has explained an idea or technique, it is a good idea to test the students to see if they have comprehended what you have presented. The fastest form of feedback is the oral drill in which you ask questions of the students randomly to determine how many are able to answer the questions you pose. Written drills at the end of class not only reenforce your oral instructions but also enable you to see if you should progress to a more complex skill in the next lesson.

3. Guest speakers — Inquiries to large corporations, police and fire departments, social agencies, universities,

science centers and museums as well as teachers and students in your own school will provide a long list of people who are qualified to speak to your group on a wide variety of subjects.

4. Film strips — Large school systems have libraries of film strips located in individual schools or in central locations which are available for use by classroom teachers. Many large corporations and businesses supply films for educational use. If the school does not have a list of these companies, you can write to them directly. It usually takes several weeks to receive these films, so it would be wise to plan ahead in placing your orders. Since in any school there are bound to be several educators teaching the same subject and grade you are, it would be a good idea to check with them to see if they would like to use the films when you are. Then you can prevent duplication of film orders.

5. Experiments which illustrate a point you have been trying to make or which show the importance of the material you have been presenting also enhance learning.

6. Oral reports by students themselves contribute to the learning experiences if the rest of the class is instructed to listen for particular bits of information. Tests or quizzes on these reports will force class members to be attentive.

7. Debates and panel discussions not only contribute to the classroom learning situation but give the pupils the incentive for individual at-home preparation. These debates can involve class members or outside authorities who might be willing to attend your classes.

8. Short plays and classroom skits can enhance the learning experiences. These plays and skits can be of three types. Some might be plays written by professionals which appear in anthologies the class has read. Others might be written by class members to illustrate events or ideas studied. A third type can be organized spontaneously by the teacher or pupils to illustrate an idea the class is studying. After reading a short story, a teacher might select five or six stu-

dents and tell them to go to the back of the room to organize a skit illustrating how the story might have ended differently if some of the characters hadn't made the choices they made or if fate hadn't intervened in their lives. After reading about the customs in France, several students might act out the scene at a French wedding or family breakfast. Others might re-create a historical moment in British history. This type of activity not only reenforces learning experiences but increases cooperative attitudes between members of the class.

9. Mimeographed supplementary materials prove invaluable in filling the voids in your textbook's drill and explanatory materials. You can use mimeographed sheets to give extra drills to pupils and save yourself from spending valuable class time drawing diagrams, writing tests, additional notes and instructions on the board.

10. Silent and oral reading is another approach which can be taken with classroom materials. Students, particularly slower students, enjoy oral reading. Many teachers resort to oral reading in classes where they experience discipline problems because, for some miraculous, unexplained reasons, noisy students seem to get quiet during periods of oral reading. Neither silent nor oral reading should be done without some check being made on the comprehension of the pupils. Oral and written questions of factual and interpretative concepts should be asked after each reading assignment. Never make silent or oral reading the only activity for the entire period. Teaching must be done before, during and after each period of silent reading to insure optimum learning.

11. Free reading enhances student learning. If you are fortunate enough to have your own classroom library or are close enough to the school library to permit easy access to the book shelves, an occasional session of free reading can prove to be very profitable. The students can be permitted to select books on subjects related to classroom studies and then report on them in writing or orally.

12. Class trips outside of the school building always arouse enthusiasm in subject matter. Visits to business firms,

historic sites, plays and movies, lectures, colleges, museums and other institutions can reenforce classroom learning experiences. Most school systems have facilities for providing transportation out of the building. Two or three of the parents of your pupils, other teachers or student-teachers should accompany you on any trips you make to help you keep track of your pupils and keep things running smoothly. Never attempt to take pupils out of the building without first securing parental permission and the blessings of school authorities.

13. Individual, small group and committee research projects can help to diversify the material presented in the classroom. If a very broad subject area is to be covered, dividing the class into small groups can save time and prevent boredom as well as give the students the opportunity to express themselves before their peers.

14. Prepare models, charts, booklets, murals, posters and graphs. You can do this yourself or the students can do it on their own. The finished products can be displayed around the room and examined by small groups of students before and after class and at certain designated times during the class period.

15. Have students work in small groups to prepare bulletin boards reflecting their classroom activities for display in one of the school corridors or in the classroom itself.

16. Watch a television program or listen to a radio broadcast which is relevant to the subject being studied. Always prepare the students for the listening experiences by telling them what they are to be listening for and what information you hope they will learn.

MATERIALS

Always plan in advance for the materials you and the students will need in order to carry out the lesson. Make a list all the materials needed when you are planning the lesson so that you can refer to it well in advance of the class period and then again at the last minute to be certain you are bringing all the supplies you need. Never assume that a tape recorder, slide projector, film strip, empty classroom, ream of paper, musical instrument, drawing paper, microscope or guest speaker will be available when you need it without making several confirmations in advance.

Be certain that you inform the students well in advance of the class period that there are certain materials which they are responsible for bringing to class. They will need frequent reminders of the needed supplies from the time you make the assignment until the time you expect them to be prepared. Warning them in advance will give them sufficient time to prepare the models, speeches, or collection of newspaper and magazine clippings you asked them to bring.

It is doubly wise to announce well in advance the materials students will be required to purchase so that they can begin saving the money needed to purchase books, tools, accessories, uniforms, tickets or any other supplies for which they must use their own funds. Be careful when you assign pupils to bring materials of their own to school that your demands are reasonable as far as availability of materials and financial resources are concerned. Students from deprived areas or with low intellectual abilities cannot be expected to travel long distances to purchase materials, interview people or visit places of interest on their own. They also cannot be expected to make purchases of materials on short notice because many will have to save or budget for needed extra purchases in advance or wait until a pay or relief check is received and cashed.

Never assume that students will have needed supplies easily available at home. Teachers who come from middle-class backgrounds are often surprised to learn how few pupils have newspapers brought into their homes daily or even on Sundays or how few have telephones and writing paper in their homes on a regular basis. Make your demands for outside materials realistic with the resources and abilities of your pupils.

CONCLUSION

The concluding activities in your lessons should fulfill two purposes. First, they should tie all of the work done that period together by restating, or requiring the pupils to reuse, the main ideas of the lesson. Ideally, the concluding activity should be brief and oral. This will enable the teacher to spot-check her pupils to determine how many in the class assimilated the material and how many will need additional review. It will indicate if the class is ready, as a group, to proceed to the next activity or whether the teacher will have to go over the same material again in the next lesson.

The concluding activities should also serve to bridge the gap into the next day's lessons. They should prepare the pupils for what is to follow by showing them the relationship between what they learned today, what they can hope to learn tomorrow and what they learned yesterday.

HOMEWORK ASSIGNMENTS

Homework assignments should not be busy work activities given to punish students for misbehavior in class. Nor should they become activities designed merely to prove to the parents that you accomplished something in class that day. Rather they should be planned to reenforce in-class activities. The homework assignment should require the students to use the skills or knowledge taught during the class period. They should reveal to the student what he actually knows and does not know about the subject matter. Many pupils honestly believe that they understand what you covered in class and are not aware of how little they know until they try to work independently. Aside from showing the pupils how much they know, the completed homework will indicate to you how much of what you have taught has penetrated and how much needs to be retaught.

Just as you established standards of deportment and requirements for in-class work, you must expect certain requirements to be met in regard to homework assignments.

All homework assignments should be done neatly and in ink, unless they are calculating mathematics problems. All homework should be done on regulation size paper. The standard size for most notebook paper is 8" by 11". If you do not emphasize this seemingly minor point, you will receive homework written on everything from the inside of a chocolate bar wrapper to the front of a lunch bag. Demand that all assignments be turned in on time or receive loss of grade points as a penalty. Employers will not accept late work. Neither should teachers. Often, if a teacher is not strict in enforcing the rules about punctuality of assignment completion, she is plagued by several hundred papers turned in the day before report card grades are due.

When you make homework assignments, always check before you give them to the class to be certain that they are accurate and fair. Recheck page numbers to see if the exercises you wanted them to do are on the pages you assigned. Students panic at midnight when they discover that the page they wrote down for their science assignment is actually a diagram of the intestinal tract of a frog. If the students were careless, they deserve to suffer. If the mistake was the teacher's, they should not have to lose a night's sleep because of your error.

Never assign work that you have not first tried to do yourself. Always try to do your own homework assignments before giving them to the class to ascertain that they are capable of being done. If you don't, you are taking a chance of having forty students desperately placing long distance calls to relatives all over the country trying to find the answer to mathematics problems which can't be solved or searching for the derivations of misspelled words which don't exist.

When you are doing your own assignments, time yourself to see how long it takes you to complete the work. Then try to judge how long it will take the pupils to do the same problems. Having been a student at one time yourself, bear in mind the fact that your subject is not the only one for which they have homework. Therefore, make your assignments reasonable in both content and length.

Knowing what your assignment is going to be in advance helps to avoid repetition of assignments and prevents the confusion which would occur at the end of a period if you are forced to devise an assignment while forty students are pushing their way toward the door in an effort to escape before you think of one. Advance preparation also prevents you from forgetting to give an assignment you wanted completed by a certain date or from having the embarrassing experience of forgetting what you assigned them to do the next day when pupils question you about their homework.

If you list your homework assignments as part of your lesson plans, you will be able to refer to them easily when you need to know what work an absent student missed. You will be able to tell easily exactly what assignment belonged with each specific classroom lesson.

Constructing well-organized lessons is extremely important to both you and your pupils. You will be considerably more relaxed in the classroom knowing that all your class time is planned for and that you know toward what ends you and your pupils are striving. You also know how you are going to guide them toward the accomplishment of worthwhile goals. Your confidence and knowledge will be conveyed to the students. They will react positively toward this confidence and will be less apt to challenge your authority or question your motives in making assignments. Occasionally, students will ask, "Why do we have to learn that? It's dumb!" Should a student pose such a question earnestly, you should answer him as clearly and honestly as you can. He has a right to know why he should learn the skills you are trying to teach him to use. Of course, you should have explained this in one way or another in your motivational exercises or in the introduction to the lesson. However, if the student has failed to understand why the material is important to him, he should be made to realize why learning it is necessary. Even if the student is not sincere in his questioning and is just trying to embarrass you or make you feel uncomfortable in front of the class, he deserves an honest explanation. His sarcastic question could very easily reflect the feelings of more polite, less extroverted pupils who would profit from your explanation of the validity of the learning goals.

Clear, concise lesson plans are of service to people other than you and your students. They enable someone to take over in your absence who may be inexperienced in your field. It will be very easy for a substitute to follow your lesson plans if you have organized them in the manner suggested above.

It will also be easier for you to assist absent students or students who know that they will be out of school for some time at a future date if you can turn to organized lessons to see what the pupil has missed or is going to miss. Notes jotted down on scrap pieces of paper and on the backs of shopping lists are most difficult to refer to. Permanent, structured lesson plans can be altered as the need arises and used for many terms. They become a permanent record of your educational goals, approaches and techniques.

Finally, your lesson plans will be helpful to administrators or visitors who attend your classes and feel the necessity for questioning new or unusual techniques or approaches you have taken with your subject matter. They will be relieved and impressed when you are able to show them the direction you intend to take clearly explained in your lesson plans. These plans can save you from making a lot of explanations and justifications when you are able to show a clear developmental program for outsiders to examine.

Planning classroom activities is one of the few educational chores the teacher is able to perform while not under pressure. While working on these plans, the teacher must acknowledge that because of the unpredictability of human behavior and the ever-present school emergencies such as fire drills and long assemblies, the chances of carrying the lessons out exactly as planned are very slim. However, if the teacher is thoroughly prepared to carry them out, relying on her intelligence and common sense and interpreting the clues she receives from her students' behavior, she will be able to make those on-the-spot changes in her plans which are necessary to insure effective and meaningful lessons.

(Denison's Teacher's Daily Plan Book, $2.25 a copy, is recommended for outlining lesson plans.)

Chapter Six

Room Decoration

New teachers tend to minimize the importance of decorating the classroom. Most educators have not been in secondary school classrooms as students for at least four years and since very few college classrooms are adorned with anything but meeting announcements, class schedules, grade reports and graffiti, they tend to feel that classroom decoration is a chore relegated to kindergarten and nursery school teachers. However, nothing could be farther from the truth.

Classroom decorations can inform and entertain. They are important as motivational tools and as educational devices. Culturally deprived and educationally disadvantaged pupils come from such drab home environments that pleasantly decorated classrooms serve as an inducement to increase class attendance. For brighter, more advanced students, classroom decorations function as educational experiences.

The average teacher, unless he or she comes from the art department or has been fortunate enough to inherit visual aids material from an older, retiring friend, feels overwhelmed by the task of classroom decoration. The lost, sinking feeling of wondering what to do with extensive bulletin board space is not necessary. There are many sources to which a teacher can go for help in making her classroom pleasant and attractive as well as educational. Some of these material sources are:

1. Local businesses and large companies which will supply posters and bulletin board materials to advertise

their products. If these products are being studied or used by your pupils, their posters can be informative as well as decorative. Book companies and research firms are also particularly good sources to contact about materials of this sort.

2. Magazine illustrations and newspaper articles which are relevant to your subject matter can be displayed in various sections of the room. With this type of decoration, student participation can be very high. Students can be of great assistance in locating articles in magazines and newspapers they receive at home or in magazines you give them to read independently. Asking students to look for magazine and newspaper articles relating to subjects the class is studying will tend to keep students thinking about what they have learned after school hours and will reenforce in-class learning experiences.

3. A section of the bulletin board space can be designated to display student work. Sections of available space should be reserved for displaying student art work relevant to a country being discussed, geometric shapes being examined, illustrations of stories read by the group, or diagrams of animals to be dissected. Students are often interested in the work done by their classmates. Test papers and homework assignments which have been done well can also be displayed in these areas.

4. Educational supply houses, located in many big cities, handle bulletin board materials for the teacher who feels financially capable of investing small sums of money. Companies which supply paper products for children's parties also handle bulletin board decorations which reflect national holidays and subjects of general interest, ready for easy mounting.

5. There is nothing to prevent the teacher from creating some original material with a scissors, crayons and construction paper if she is artistic and has some extra time.

6. A home-made calendar showing school events and holidays is an easy decoration to make and one to which students refer frequently.

7. Charts showing assignments completed, grades reached and assignments due can be posted on segments of the bulletin board space for easy reference by students.

Most of these decorations can be prepared quickly and without too much effort on the part of the teacher. These simple decorating steps are not being suggested merely to enable the teacher to take the easy way out, or to encourage her to avoid one of her responsibilities. However, the new teacher must be practical. There are so many things a novice must do that the more she simplifies duties such as these, the more time she will have to spend on lesson planning and getting to know her students and the school routine.

In preparing classroom decorations several important items should be taken into consideration.

1. The decorations should reflect the subject matter of your course or the students' immediate social and educational interests. Be careful that the illustrations are not too juvenile for your pupils or are beyond their levels of understanding.

2. The over-all appearance of the room should be cheerful and inviting. Pupils should feel comfortable and pleased by their surroundings. Your room may well be the one bright place in their lives and could provide a welcome relief from the dreary homes from which they come.

3. A way to display your pupils' work and report on their achievements should be included in your decorating plans. These accomplishments can reflect individual or group work in educational or social areas as in charts reflecting the amount of money or supplies collected by pupils for charity drives or in the form of test papers and well-written homework assignments. Remember that in displaying students' work or reports on students' achievements, you should only be reflecting their accomplishments, not their failings. Never embarrass students by posting a report of the entire class' grades which includes those who failed or came close to fail-

ing. You do more harm in embarrassing the failures than you achieve in rewarding the successes.

4. Pupils should be encouraged to contribute to the decorations as much as possible. Even students who are not very intelligent, skilled or artistic can be called upon to tack up background materials or cut out pictures and block letters. This will tend to give potential decoration-destroyers and mutilators a sense of responsibility and a feeling of belonging.

5. Be certain that all pictures and illustrations are mounted neatly and fastened securely. Curling corners are irresistible temptations to students who cannot refrain from pulling on them. Uneven drawings distract pupils and draw their attention away from you.

6. Printed material and pictures, particularly headings and titles, should be large enough to be seen through the entire room. Illustrations which cannot be seen and titles which cannot be read are defeating their own purposes.

7. Change decorations frequently. After materials have been displayed for more than a week or two, students no longer notice they are there and they become ineffective. Before this happens, it is time for a change.

8. Try to vary the type of decorations you use as much as possible. One week you might display posters describing a country being studied and a few weeks later replace them with student photographs of a class trip to a historical site. These might be followed by newspaper clippings relating to an area being studied. A mathematics teacher might hang up newspaper articles discussing the use of mathematics in research and follow these by a general display depicting cartoons from a local magazine illustrating the effects of the generation gap. Decorations do not always have to relate only to your subject area. General displays can be functional also.

9. Be careful not to use objects which might be harmful to the students' well-being. Displaying a war souvenir, pointed compass or glass or small objects which are easily thrown at classmates is asking for trouble which you are most certain to receive.

10. The message of the display must be clearly stated and easily understood. In most cases, the title or heading should contain only a few words posted in bold letters. The relationship between the objects or items shown should be clearly understandable. If the students cannot understand bulletin board materials, they will ignore them rather than ask you what you mean so that their educational contribution is negated.

11. Always proofread your bulletin boards to eliminate spelling and grammar errors. Occasionally, a teacher will purposely insert a spelling or grammar error designed to attract a class' attention or to try to build a warm teacher-student relationship by showing the class how human the teacher is. Some educators think this is cute. In reality, however, it is extremely poor practice because displaying incorrect information reenforces misconceptions. Later, pupils can't remember how to spell a word correctly or decide which grammatical form to use because they saw both forms in print and cannot remember which is the correct one.

CONCLUSION

Cheerful informative surroundings make the learning process more enjoyable for you and the students. It is unquestionably more desirable for all concerned to work in a pleasant cheerful environment. The amount of work a teacher has to expend in order to create pleasant surroundings is far surpassed by the increased student interest and positive reactions exhibited to you, your subject matter and your classroom.

Chapter Seven

Individual Differences

The controversy over whether homogeneous or heterogeneous grouping is more conducive to intellectual and social growth seems to loom as a perpetual educational problem. Some educators feel that grouping students heterogeneously inspires slower students to achieve their highest potentials because of their exposure to their more intelligent and highly-motivated peers. The better students, it is felt, are not held back because the effective teacher meets their needs with extra instruction and assignments. Rapid learners benefit from the social insight and training they receive. Since the intellectually superior person does not exist in a social vacuum, many schools hope heterogeneous grouping will teach the better pupil to relate to his slower comrades while still functioning on his own superior level.

Although this type of grouping might work well in small school districts where the average teacher has approximately fifteen (15) pupils per class, in large urban school systems, teachers cannot cope effectively with 40-50 pupils who exhibit diverse needs and abilities. Therefore, the tendency in urban areas is to group pupils as homogeneously as possible on the basis of standardized test scores and/or curriculum choices.

Even though many schools make a decided effort to group their pupils homogeneously, the large numbers of students attending city schools result in great ranges in pupil ability and interest in every classroom. It then becomes the teacher's responsibility to make provisions for these wide ranges in individual ability and interest within the context of her lesson plans. Even small classes in which the students have selected a common course of study directed toward accomplishing the same goal of college admission or preparation for a trade contain wide ranges in pupil ability and interest. It is extremely important that the teacher recognize that these differences exist, identify the extent of these variations and find ways of coping with the disparages in potential. If a student's interests are not being satisfied or if the work is too far above or below his ability, he will lose any desire he might have had to learn and will become a potentially disruptive force in the classroom. More tragic than this is the fact that if he sees that there is nothing for him in your lessons, he will miss out on all the education he might have gotten if you had been able to meet his educational needs.

PROVISIONS FOR DIFFERENCES IN ABILITY

The more difficult problems in coping with individual differences arise in providing for ranges of ability. A child who is very intelligent and quite skilled in dealing with mathematical concepts and scientific theories may be totally unable to pronounce a French phrase clearly or write a well-organized theme. Since most groupings are based upon standardized intelligence tests, variations in special abilities are not provided for. Therefore, the classroom teacher must plan to deal with these variations in each of the lessons she presents. There are several relatively easy ways for her to meet these needs without taking valuable classroom time away from the majority of the pupils whose capabilities do fall within a rather narrow range of abilities. For the minority, the teacher can make the following provisions:

1. Provide extra outside reading lists or study sheets for those students who finish their assignments before the rest of their classmates or who find the work too difficult for them to do. This will enable both groups of pupils—the superior and the inferior—to proceed at their own rates of

learning without having to wait for their classmates to catch up to their levels or falling hopelessly behind themselves.

2. In every assignment made and in every test given, include some problems and examples which enable slower pupils to experience success and learning reenforcement. Also include a few which will challenge the more advanced students. This necessitates wide ranges in the type and complexity of each exercise.

3. Try to work out a system which will enable those who finish their classwork early to help those who are having difficulty. The arrangements for this sort of activity should be handled tactfully in order to avoid inflating the egos of the advanced and embarrassing the slow. A working system can be set up privately between the students and the teacher after class. Those who are going to be working together should be seated close to each other so that there won't be any obvious or disruptive movements near the conclusion of each classwork assignment.

4. Hold after-school conferences to give help to those who are having difficulty grasping your subject or to suggest extra work to challenge the better students. This technique will not only provide the obvious benefit of encouraging students to do extra work and achieve their innate potentials, but your interest will illustrate to the pupils that their teacher is concerned with assisting her students as individuals. This will motivate the pupils to strive for higher goals as they attempt to justify your personal interest in them.

5. Use the home which can prove to be a rich source of outside help for students who exhibit ability differences. Many families are well aware of their children's abilities and are anxious to help the substandard or superior child to achieve his full potential. Unfortunately, most families do not know how to give constructive help. Letters or phone calls to parents or older brothers and sisters suggesting activities and drills which might be done at home under the direction of lay people to increase learning of pupils at both ends of

95

the achievement scale will be appreciated and be very helpful to the learners and the teacher.

6. In conjunction with the above suggestion, the teacher should make herself aware of professionals within the school and tutors outside of the school who can deal with the high and low ability of pupils on an individual basis. Foundations, colleges, social action groups and other nonprofit organizations often establish programs to help pupils after school. Teachers can contact these groups personally or through the guidance counselor or principal. Large school systems usually hire reading and speech therapists to work with pupils on an individual basis. Your school administration office can tell you how to contact these people.

7. Grouping students into ability groups within each class is another way to handle large variations in ability. After giving instruction to each group, the teacher should circulate throughout the room and supervise and assist the work of each group.

8. When the opportunity presents itself, allow the better students to work independently on individualized projects while you give personal attention to lower ability pupils. You can vary this procedure to give you time to work with the superior students while the slower children are doing some personalized work.

While the teacher should make every effort she can to help students on an individualized basis, she must be very careful not to emphasize the ability differences in the class or castigate those of lower ability while praising the more successful. All provisions for meeting ability differentials should be administered tactfully and discreetly. Students are more aware of their capabilities and inadequacies than we realize. They know who the superior and inferior students are and they know exactly where they fit in. Granting the same respect and attention to those chores completed by the slower students that is given to those done by the faster ones will encourage the inferior ones to work harder and help erase unnecessary feelings of anxiety and shame. All lessons should

96

include some way for the slow students to achieve an element of success even if you have to use some "give-away questions" with obvious answers.

PROVISIONS FOR DIFFERENCES IN INTEREST

Regardless of how intelligent or motivated a pupil is, if his interests are not being aroused, he will not have any desire to learn your subject matter and his accomplishments and achievements will decline or become nonexistent. He is as likely to become a dropout as his counterpart whose ability needs are not being met. In order to prevent this student-potential loss, there are several procedures a teacher can follow to provide for the interest variations found within any classroom situation.

1. Research projects and interviews conducted outside of class give pupils the opportunity to develop and satisfy individual interests. Oral reports made to the entire class and private discussions students have in the halls and lunch-rooms give pupils the opportunity to share their interests with classmates and hopefully even transmit their enthusiasm and interests to others.

2. Provisions in individual reading assignments should enable students to exercise freedom of choice. Allow pupils to select outside reading material from a wide list of relevant works.

3. Invite guest speakers into the classroom and plan outside trips which help to foster the growth and expansion of individual interests. If you teach in a large urban school system, you will be surprised to find how few pupils have ever traveled outside of their own neighborhood to visit places of interest in other parts of the city.

4. Group projects will enable students to develop and use their individual interests and will give them the opportunity to share their knowledge with the rest of their group and their classmates.

5. Establish a variety of goals toward which the students can strive. The entire class does not have to work toward the same ends or at the same rate of speed.

6. Display models, pamphlets, pictures and diagrams which relate to your subject matter to arouse student interest in the many facets of your subject area. A trade preparatory student who hates mathematics and thinks science is useless for him might be stimulated to learn how to select the best gasoline for his car and how to calculate gasoline mileage using a mathematical formula. This type of individualized planning takes a little longer to do but the returns are well worth your time investment.

The majority of your pupils, no matter how mature or intelligent, come into your classroom with a "so what?" attitude. In order to have their cooperation, you must find a way to answer their "so what?" They must be shown that the subject has something of value to offer them. They have to see that you are trying to teach them something that they can use in their daily lives or something which arouses their curiosities and spikes their imaginations. If they are not made to realize the importance of your subject, they are almost certain to become learning dropouts. They will start to cut your class and turn you off when they are physically present. It is extremely difficult to win back the confidence and attention of students once they have been lost. The most certain way to insure your success as a teacher is to educate your pupils to achieve their potentials by reaching all of their needs. The only way to accomplish this very difficult feat is to meet the needs of the many intellectually and culturally diverse human beings in your classroom through the use of the techniques which have been suggested here.

Chapter Eight

Every Teacher as a Reading Teacher

At the secondary school level, every subject matter teacher should also be a reading teacher. Potential learning problems often spring from reading disabilities. These problem learners are the most likely candidates to become school dropouts. A student who cannot read his science or social studies textbooks with understanding is not able to comprehend the main ideas of the texts. As a result, he loses interest in the subject itself and finally becomes a school dropout, or at least a classroom dropout.

Even the better, more advance students evidence reading problems if they do not have profitable prereading instruction and assistance. These pupils do their reading assignments faithfully but find that they cannot remember what they have read a few minutes after they have completed their assignment. They must read a section three or four times in order to answer simple contextual questions and find it difficult to make any reasonable value judgments based upon their reading.

In order to prevent problems in comprehension from occurring in your subject area, it is necessary that you teach your pupils how to read your textbooks and then give them reading instruction before each reading assignment. One of the most efficient and effective ways to give reading instruction is through the Directed Reading Activities Approach.

THE DIRECTED READING ACTIVITIES APPROACH

The DRA approach to reading instruction has proven to be one of the more successful approaches to reading instruction at the secondary school level. The basic concept of the program rests upon the idea that students must be prepared in advance for the subject matter they are to read. The classroom teacher prepares the students in the following manner:

1. Be certain that the students understand the title of the book, article, essay or short story that they are going to read. Explain, or ask the students to explain, the title of the work they are going to read. Ask them to tell you what they expect to be taught on the basis of reading the title. Explain any abstract terms in the titles with which the students might not be familiar and give them the opportunity to supply examples of their own to illustrate their understanding of the meaning.

2. After they are acquainted with the title and understand its relationship to the work, list the new and difficult vocabulary words or terms the students are going to encounter in their reading. Go over the meanings and pronunciations of the words before the students read the selection. Having them read passages in which they cannot recognize or understand the key words or phrases is a waste of time leading to frustration and boredom.

3. Work with the students on the use of context clues to help them determine the meaning of words they do not recognize. Put some sentences on the board or refer to some in their textbooks to show students how to supply the meaning to words or phrases they don't understand from the rest of the sentence. You can begin to explain how to use context clues by putting simple sentences on the board such as:

John went to the store for his mother to buy a .... of milk to pour on his .... and a pound of .... to spread on his ....
Mary's .... sister tore pages out of her homework .... so Mary .... her.

Make the students realize that when they do not understand a word they can make a rather good guess about its meaning from the rest of the sentence. Show them how to do this by selecting specific sentences from their texts containing new words or phrases and demonstrate how they can interpret the new information based on the words around it.

4. Prepare the students for the selection or chapter to be read by telling them something about the section and giving them some questions they have to answer in their reading. For example tell the class that:

"Today we are going to read a story about a boy who tries to escape a problem by running away from home. In the beginning of the story we are told what his problem is and why he feels he has to run away. See if you can find out what his problem is, where he runs and who the first person he meets is."

or

"Open your books to the section on frogs. The first few paragraphs tell how the frog is like a smaller animal we studied last week. It also tells us what provisions the frog is able to make to adapt to its environment. Read the first two pages to find out what other animals the frog is like, how it is like this animal and what both animals must do to prepare for winter weather."

5. After a sufficient period of silent reading has elapsed, have the students pause in their reading to answer oral questions. These questions should be the specific ones you asked them to look for in their reading combined with some additional deeper questions in which you require them to assimilate the material and make some predictions for the future. Your discussion might take the following form:

"Now that you've found out that Johnny meets a policeman shortly after he runs away, what do you think is going to happen to him? Will they send him home or can he fool the policeman into thinking that he has his parents' permission to be out so late? How do you think he can overcome his problems with his father?"

or

"Now that you've read about how the frog prepares for winter, what preparations do you think
he makes for summer months? What larger animals have the same problems he does?"

Then have the students finish reading to find out if their
answers are correct.

6. If the size of the class and the nature of the assignment permit, allow the students to finish reading silently
and then have them answer detailed questions orally and
in writing. Their written answers can be done at the end of
the reading assignment with the oral work following, or the
plan can be alternated.

7. If you are working with a piece of literature, you
might spend some time at the conclusion of the period having
the students read orally. Never ask students to read orally
unless they have first read the material silently and you are
certain that they have comprehended what they have read.

8. When the entire section has been read silently and
any oral reading you might want to do has been completed,
follow each reading session by factual questions which determine the amount of the pupils' comprehension. Then ask
questions which require the class to use the information to
make value judgments or to group facts together to form
generalized meaningful concepts.

9. Make later referrals to the materials the class has
read and to new words and skills the pupils have learned.
This will further reenforce positive reading skills.

10. It is often desirable to have secondary school pupils
keep a notebook or list of new vocabulary terms learned in
the course of their reading activities. These lists can be made
up of new words you give them at the beginning of each
exercise and of words they come across while they are reading individually. The words should be reviewed periodically
to be certain they are not forgotten.

The teacher must constantly be aware of the danger
signs of reading difficulty so that problems can be met and

dealt with quickly. Many of these problems can be handled by the classroom teacher. Others, if they indicate that the pupils involved are very inferior in ability should be referred to reading specialists for trained outside assistance. Those with minor problems can be given extra help by the classroom teacher during her conference periods, while the class is working on group problems or while the rest of the class is reading silently.

Some of the signs of reading difficulties for which the classroom teacher should be aware are:

1. Use of fingers or markers to point to the reader's place
2. Movement of lips during silent reading
3. Distracted easily by noise or students around him
4. Constant refusals to read silently and orally
5. Sub-vocalizing of material in silent reading
6. Completing reading assignment long after the rest of the class
7. Inability to answer factual or judgmental questions on material read
8. Repeated assertions that a pupil "doesn't want to read" or "doesn't like to read"
9. Forgetting of books on a chronic basis

All of the above, individually or in combinations are indications of reading problems. Many English teachers are trained to cope with these problems themselves. However, teachers in other subject areas should be on the alert for these problems and refer them to the reading teacher, if the school system employs one, or to the English teacher for immediate action.

While the problem reader needs the added attention of qualified reading specialists, all students need to have their reading directed in the manner suggested by the Directed Reading Approach. Telling pupils to read Chapter 4 of their history textbook or pages 27 to 38 of their Chemistry book is not teaching. Most students will come into class the next day remembering nothing of what they read the night before. All students must be directed to read to learn something specific. They have to be given the opportunity to do the reading and then be checked to see that they have comprehended and can use what they have read in a practical manner. This form of reading instruction is simple enough to be used in every classroom by every subject matter teacher on an entire class basis. It does require that the teacher do more preparation than simply selecting and assigning a reading selection. However, the returns the educator receives in the form of positive learning results are more than worth the time expenditure on the teacher's part.

Chapter Nine

Techniques for Teaching Slow Learners

Every school system, regardless of its location or the affluence of its constituents, has its share of students who are classified as "slow learners." These pupils are not retarded. Retarded students are usually segregated in special schools or special classes with trained teachers who are qualified to cope with their unique learning difficulties. However, slow pupils do have learning abilities and potentials which are considerably below those of the average school population. Unfortunately for both these pupils and for novice educators, bright classes and advanced students are traditionally awarded to the most experienced teachers by department heads and principals as rewards for faithful or excellent service. This means that most new and inexperienced teachers are likely to find that they have at least one "slow" class on their teaching schedule, if not an entire roster composed of such groups. The irony of this situation is that the teaching of slow learners requires experience, insight, patience and skill which most beginning teachers do not possess. The seasoned educators who do have these talents are often exempted from the "slow rosters" by virtue of their seniority. The frustrations of teaching for the first time are compounded when the new teacher faces a class of slow learners and tries to communicate with them without insulting them or alienating them by presenting material which is too juvenile or too difficult for them.

The term "slow learners" is a very ambiguous one and is hard to define because what a school district may classify as "slow" in an affluent suburban school district may be termed "average" in an inner-city district. It would be wise, therefore, for the beginning teacher to examine the cumulative records of her prospective pupils before the semester begins or as close to the beginning of the term as possible. These records will give you information on the standardized test scores of your pupils. Most schools group the pupils into sections on the basis of their I.Q. scores and their reading levels as reflected in standardized reading tests. Examinations of these records will tell the teacher many facts which will help her to meet the needs of her pupils satisfactorily. These records are usually centrally located in the school and, in most instances, you will be able to skim through these reports in fifteen or twenty minutes. The time invested will prove to be well worth your effort because the knowledge you gain from these records about your students' capabilities and potentials will make lesson planning more meaningful and rewarding for you and your classes.

The cumulative records will indicate how wide a range of ability exists in your class. Ways of coping with these differences in ability have been suggested in an earlier chapter. Knowing which students are the probable low achievers and which have the potential for assimilating more difficult tasks is helpful in enabling the teacher to meet these needs in her lesson preparations. However, she must be careful not to allow the information she reads in these records to prejudice her view of her pupils. Fixing a student in your mind as a nonachiever or as a strong candidate for failure is deadly for the pupil and for your chances of effectiveness. Some pupils are repeatedly classified into groups in which they do not belong because of their inability to perform well in standardized tests. The wise teacher is one who is always on the alert for such students. Likewise, a teacher who demands too much of a pupil on the basis of standardized test results is in danger of causing harm to a pupil's development. A child who is asked to achieve above his capabilities gives up trying very easily and is frustrated to the point of dropping out of class if not out of school altogether.

Checking the cumulative records will also give the prospective teacher some insight into other reasons for pupils' failures to achieve subject-matter proficiency. Comments about broken homes, physical defects, financial deprivations, previous educational difficulties and ill health will help the educator to deal with the individual problems of her pupils.

All of the rules of good lesson planning and maintaining classroom discipline and control apply to the slow learner as they do to all classes. However, planning for the slow learner is more difficult. This is due in part to the scarcity of suitable materials for slow students. Since most slow students read at grade levels which are several steps below their chronological grade levels, the materials which are suitable to their interest-levels will be too difficult for them to read with understanding. Furthermore, those books which they can read coherently will often be illustrated with juvenile pictures and diagrams or printed in the large letters or numbers associated with the capabilities of students several grades below the ones in which they are. As soon as your classes encounter such texts their reactions are almost certain to be—"That's a baby book. We ain't gonna read that!" If the school in which you are teaching does not have a supply of books and materials which meet the interest levels of slow learners written at levels at which they can function, it will be necessary for the teacher to produce many of her own instructional aides. The new teacher should be prepared for this inevitability because, until recently, school districts pretended that slow learners did not exist or that they constituted so small a portion of the school population that it was unnecessary to invest funds in purchasing special supplies suited to their needs. Publishing companies reflected their disinterest by publishing few texts or materials designed to meet the needs of these students. The advent of the launching of Sputnik by the Russians in the 1950s directed the attention of the nation toward the rapid, intellectually advanced, college-bound pupil with such force that the needs of the slow learners were virtually overlooked or ignored.

While this situation has been improving steadily, most schools have a great deficit in readily available materials for slower learners. This is caused not only by the fact that the stockpiles of teaching aides for students of this type were negligible to begin with but also because of the reluctance of school boards and parents' groups to delegate funds for purchases for slow classes. Parents' groups prefer to pretend that slow learners do not exist and that when they do, their needs are small. Therefore, you must be prepared to spend a great deal of time constructing special materials for your slow learners. You might even have to rewrite your textbooks by simplifying explanations and adding examples and diagrams to make the reading material understandable and appealing. You should also be constantly alert for things outside the classroom which might appeal to your slow learners. Experienced teachers will confess that years in the classroom have turned them into "pack rats." Novelty place mats from restaurants containing math problems, poems, and brain teasers are good sources for motivational or supplementary material for slow learners. Advertising brochures, airplane travel booklets and stories from magazines you or your family receive will help to supplement your assigned texts and the materials you have written for your classes yourself.

There are many steps the educator must take in order to secure effective learning on the part of slow learners in addition to seeing to it that proper learning equipment such as books and magazines are made available by you personally or by the school. More than any other student, the slow learner needs the security offered by an established, definite, daily classroom routine and clear set of rules and regulations. Permanent seats should be assigned as early as possible in the beginning of the semester and pupils must be required to maintain those seats unless behavioral problems or physical difficulties require the teacher, not the students themselves, to make changes. Insisting that the pupils take their assigned seats against their will sounds dictatorial but it has its basis in good educational practice. Not only will keeping students in their assigned seats enable you to learn their names quickly and check attendance easily but it will prevent friends from distracting and annoying each other. If you do not make a point of requiring pupils to take their assigned seats from the beginning of the term, you will find that they are not only changing seats daily but are sliding from one seat to another during your lesson. If this should occur after you have stressed the importance of staying in the correct seats in a private discussion with the movable pupil, stop your lesson and do not begin to teach again until the student moves back to his correct seat. If you allow pupils to move while you are teaching, you will end up with a very animated, but inattentive classroom.

Explain the rules and regulations for classroom procedures clearly. Keep the classroom regulations as brief as possible, but be certain that those regulations you do establish are followed daily. You must be firm but not rigid. Should a regulation prove to be impractical or too difficult for your pupils to carry out, do not hesitate to cancel or rescind your orders. Keep these regulations brief, enforceable and posted in a place in the classroom which can be referred to readily and which is easily visible.

Require that necessary equipment such as pencils, textbooks and notebooks be brought to class daily. Slow learners find it difficult enough to keep their mind on classroom activities without the added distraction of having to borrow supplies or share books with other pupils. Although slow learners cannot do the work at the level of their more average peers, they can be trained to bring their educational implements to class daily. Even pupils in the elementary grades are expected to do this. If you do not insist upon this, you will spend the first half of every class period distributing pencils, paper, pens and extra textbooks from your supply closet.

Use your blackboard space to best advantage. Have the program for the day written on the board. Go over the steps in the day's lesson with the pupils at the beginning of the period so that they know in what direction they are heading with the classroom activities. Invite them to question anything they do not understand. These steps will be helpful in enabling those students whose attentions have wandered to find their way back to the classroom activities with a minimum of difficulty. They can check the blackboard for the steps in the day's lesson and try to find their place without disturbing everyone around them including you.

Never cover your entire blackboard area with lengthy written directions, assignments or information. Slow students find a board filled with writing overwhelming and discouraging. Rather than trying to decipher or comprehend the material, they are more apt to give up completely and ignore you and the blackboard while turning to daydreaming or disruptive behavior instead. Only write a few key ideas on the board and then expound on them orally or with supplementary material.

Slower students should have homework assignments daily which reflect and reinforce the daily classroom learning activities. They are more apt to successfully complete short daily homework assignments than long-range work. Be certain that the directions for completing the work are clear and simple and that the work is something the pupils are capable of doing without additional instruction or help from people at home. Many slow students do not have the benefit of older brothers and sisters or parents who are capable of helping them with homework assignments. This is not due, in many cases, to a lack of interest on the part of the family but to a lack of ability or time. It is beneficial, therefore, to include a sample problem to help those students who do not remember how the work was done in class refresh their memories when they must complete their lessons at home without assistance.

Choose the homework assignments carefully so that you do not make them any longer than necessary to accomplish the purpose for which they were intended. Many slow students come from deprived homes in which they must perform household chores or hold down jobs after school. This cuts into the amount of time they have available for homework considerably. Often, if a student sees that a homework assignment is so long that he has no hope of being able to complete it, he will give up without even attempting it. Therefore, be certain that the amount of work that you expect a slow child to do is reasonable. You can judge what is reasonable by seeing how long it takes your pupils to finish in-class exercises. Try not to make your homework assignment longer than twenty minutes to a half an hour. Remember that your students have three or four subjects other than yours for which they must also do homework and that their attention spans are relatively short.

If you do give slow pupils a long-range assignment, such as a book report or an independent research project, you must remind them periodically that they should be working on the assignment and that the due date is rapidly approaching. This should be done orally as well as in writing. Post a notice of the assignment requirements and the due date on a bulletin board or blackboard. It is also wise to check on the progress of the assignment periodically before it is due to be collected. For example, if you have assigned a research report on the customs of a country, the dress of a particular century, the life of a famous author or musician, or have asked the pupils to make a poster or display, a few days after the assignment has been given ask every pupil to write his exact topic on a piece of paper and submit it to you for your approval. A few days later you might ask the students to bring in the names of the books they are going to use or the materials from which they are going to make their posters and a list of the sources from which they hope to obtain these resources.

111

A week later you might ask to read their rough copies or out-lines for their assignments. Finally, a week later you can ask for the finished projects. This will not only guide the pupils in the methods to be followed for working steadily on a project for which they have been allotted a prolonged period of time, but it will enable you to see if the students are progressing in their work in a suitable manner and will enable you to help direct their work if they are not progressing in a proper manner.

Always keep an up-to-date assignment book available in an accessible place. This is a good idea for all classes, but it is even more important in slow classes where the rate of student absenteeism is more likely to be high and where the prob-ability of their phoning or consulting reliable peers to get missed assignments is low. Having a constantly-available source from which to check missed assignments will cut down, but never totally eliminate, unpreparedness and incomplete assignments.

Even more than average or above-average pupils, the slow students desperately need an established routine they can follow and rely upon. Many of them come from such chaotic home situations that the only stable environment they come in contact with is the one they find in their school classrooms. The slower and more immature a child is, the less able he is to adapt to sudden and unexpected alterations in classroom routines. This means that supplies and books used for the slow students and methods followed for distribut-ing these articles should remain the same for every lesson. If books are distributed by passing them across the rows from left to right and are collected from right to left, this procedure should be followed every time the books are used.

The same principle applies to lesson planning. If you are using the alternating method of planning rather than the unit approach, your testing days should remain constant, your days for oral work should remain the same as should your days for written work. This will not only make it easier for absent students to be prepared for work on the day they return but it will make it much easier for students to remember which books and supplies to bring to class daily. In their often chaotic lives, these slow learners need the security of knowing on which days to expect to perform specific chores. This does not mean, of course, that if a class becomes enthusiastic about an activity that it should not be continued into the next day just because the next day is usually a testing day or a drill work day. Stimulating learning activities should be continued as long as interest remains high. However, the closer a teacher of slow learners adheres to a rigid pattern of activity the more likely she is to have her pupils prepared for work and the less likely it is that chaos and confusion will occur.

The teacher of the slow learner should constantly bear in mind the significance of the term "slow learner." As the term designates, the students in such groups are capable of learning but do so at a slower rate than their peers. Therefore, as with all classes, the teacher must set reasonable standards of work and insist that they be met. It is not unreasonable to insist that all work be done neatly and carefully. Homework should be done in ink, unless students are working on maps or mathematics problems. Homework papers should be a uniform size and arranged in any pattern you establish. For example, writing their names and section number in the upper right-hand corner and the date and assignment number or title in the upper left-hand corner is a fairly standard pattern to establish. Recognition should be given for careful work, while lower marks assigned for careless work. Sloppily-done assignments should not be accepted under any circumstances and lower grades should be given for careless work. Homework assignments stained with pizza sauce or done on scraps of paper are an insult to the teacher and to the student himself. Accepting such work is an indication on your part that you feel that such work is the best that the student is capable of doing. Any student, no matter how slow, is capable of learning to be neat and careful. Prospective employers will not accept sloppy work and neither should you.

Repetitive drills of new skills and opportunities for practicing these skills in a variety of situations should be included in every lesson plan aimed at slow learners. The lower mental ability pupil needs and likes to do drill work. However, drill work should always be constructed for a definite purpose. It is not an escape device for a tired teacher who wishes to sit behind her desk and rest for a few minutes in the middle of class. All drill work should be supervised and corrected. While drill work is being done the teacher should circulate throughout the room to check that pupils are doing the work correctly and to assist those who are having difficulties. Drill work should be corrected orally or graded by the pupils themselves or by the teacher and later returned to the pupils. It should not be thrown into the "circular file" or overlooked as if it were unimportant.

The low-ability pupil has an extremely short attention span. The educator, therefore, should be on the alert for wandering attention and lack of concentration. Sometimes a teacher can renew a pupil's interest by calling on him to answer a question, read a problem orally, or give his opinion about an issue under consideration. Raising your voice or changing its tone will often renew the attention of a distracted student. Quietly walking over and standing near the chair of an inattentive pupil without stopping your lesson will often help to bring him back to the classroom activities without disrupting the rest of the class or calling attention to his inattentiveness.

Because of the inability of slower students to concentrate on any single activity for a prolonged period of time, it is important to vary the learning activities taking place each period as much as possible. Lesson planning for the slow learner should involve as many different techniques as possible without creating havoc in the classroom. This does not mean that the teacher should try to have the students switch from working quietly at their desks to using a classroom library to doing group work to reciting all in one class session. What it does mean is that slower pupils, at any grade level, should not be expected to read silently, write a composition, do drill work, or listen to oral reports or lectures for an entire period. Lessons for slow learners should include a variety of activities for each class meeting which students and teachers can alternate without creating too much confusion and chaos in the classroom. A teacher might begin the class by posing some mathematic problems or questions, then proceeding to explain a new technique for solving the problems, giving the pupils an opportunity to read the directions in the text and finally trying the problems silently. Then she can go over the problems orally with the class. In such a situation, the students have listened, read, worked silently and then participated in oral work. All of these activities involve no physical movement on the students' part, but they do require the teacher to change from one activity to the other smoothly. Such alternation of teaching techniques will help to offset boredom and lack of attention. The low mental ability pupil is frequently characterized by his fondness for routine work and a rigidity which makes it difficult for him to shift independently from one task to another. This is why the teacher must have prepared detailed lesson plans in advance which enable her to guide her pupils easily from one task to another to prevent both boredom and unnecessary activity.

One of the most difficult problems in dealing with the slow learner is overcoming the pupil's sense of inferiority. Most slow learners know that they are functioning below the rest of the school community. They have lived with defeat and failure for so long that they are programmed not to expect success. Many do not even try to achieve because they feel that they are doomed before they begin. It is necessary for every teacher of slow learners to work consciously to overcome this feeling on the part of her students and to prove to them that she does not regard them as failures and has not classified them as "hopeless" before the term's work even begins. Giving recognition for careful work and devising assignments that make it possible for the less able pupils to achieve some measure of success will give the pupils a real sense of accomplishment which will, in turn, encourage them to try harder and achieve their fullest potential. Slow learners frequently come into the classroom with a "Why try? We always flunk anyway. Don't you know we're the dummies?" attitude which the educator must work to overcome if she is to be effective. Slow learners, as a group, receive less recognition and praise than any other sector of the school community. Except for the few who excel in sports activities, music or art, they never receive commendation or respect from their peers or their teachers. One way to remedy this and to motivate the pupils is to organize class projects as the culmination of a unit of study which will enable them to show off their skills. Rex-o-graphing the six or seven best compositions or displaying the best sketches and inviting the principal and department head to see them perform are examples of ways to motivate and reward slow learners. It gives them something to strive for as well as something to be proud of. A side benefit of such activities is the satisfaction you and your superiors will receive from seeing proof of the successes of your below-average students.

Rewards for good work should be immediate and frequent. Some rewards can take the form of verbal commendations for correct answers or written notations on individual test papers indicating "good idea," "interesting point of view," "well done" or any longer notation which the teacher feels is appropriate. Motivation of the slow learner is difficult but vital. The teacher should, therefore, be on the alert for those things which her pupils find particularly enjoyable for use as motivating and rewarding devices for class-wide use. Allowing students to use the classroom library or hold group discussions or read orally can be rewards for drill work which is done correctly. A trip to a museum, visitation from a guest speaker or a film presentation might be used as a reward for a unit completed satisfactorily. Students will often indicate their preferences for certain activities by stamping their feet, booing, hissing and throwing things around the room to indicate their displeasure. The process of elimination should indicate what they do like or at least are willing to tolerate.

CONCLUSION

The first years of teaching can be very discouraging but they can also be extremely rewarding and satisfying. The moments of depression and exhilaration are magnified when the teacher is dealing with low ability pupils. This is due to the fact that they tend to be less attentive, greater disciplinary problems, capable of achieving less, and frequently less willing to cooperate with the teacher. Yet, when a teacher has been able to break through the boundaries the slow learner has set up between himself, the school and the teacher, she can make a tremendous educational contribution and reap great personal satisfaction.

Chapter Ten

Handling Interpersonal Relationships

If a teacher is to be successful in the classroom situation, she must be able to function effectively within the total school environment. In order to do this, the novice has to learn to be a diplomat as well as an educator. A teacher, if she is to be happy in her position while being an asset to her pupils and the school system which employs her, should discover ways to get along with all factions of the school community. Having a strong foundation in subject matter and educational theory is insufficient to assure the prospective teacher of success in the classroom or school at large. The new educator must find or make a place for herself within the secondary school in relation to peers, principals, parents, secretaries and custodial staff as well as securing a positive relationship with her students. This is no easy feat but it is as vital to the welfare of the teacher herself as it is to those with whom she must work. A teacher spends the major part of her waking hours in the school. Being unhappy in her job will affect every aspect of her personal life. It is to the educator's best interest to develop positive relationships with all members of the school community. Even if getting along with one's associates requires the novice to sacrifice some of her idealism and principles, the benefits to be gained by positive relationships with others far surpass the conscience-bending the newcomer will have to do.

The new teacher must remember that her classroom does not exist in a vacuum. Everything she does or fails to do affects the total school program as well as her status as a teacher. Urban high schools are often so large that the number of people with whom the teacher must deal daily is almost staggering. Those entering the teaching profession for the first time are psychologically prepared only to cope with their students. They are not aware of the vast number of people within each school who are encountered by the teacher each day in her attempts to convey some knowledge to her pupils.

RELATIONSHIPS WITH PEERS

Experienced teachers and novices share the same basic goals. They are in the schools for essentially the same reasons. Both wish to communicate as much as they can about their chosen areas of specialization and about functioning effectively in society in general in as pleasant an environment as possible. Cooperating with peers can do much to make these goals easier to accomplish.

New teachers often come into a school filled with revolutionary innovative teaching techniques. They are quick to condemn prevailing educational theories and experienced teachers for perpetuating outmoded educational methods and for student failures to achieve scholastic proficiency. Often novices are extremely vocal in their condemnation. For obvious reasons, their criticisms lodge a big wedge between them and their more experienced peers. In essence, what newcomers are doing when they criticize established procedures and tested techniques is to call their elders failures, and to negate years of hard work, faithful service and dedication on the part of those who have been with the system for one, two or possibly even more decades.

It would be wise for the new teacher to realize that an educational institution which has been in existence since long before she was born must have some things of value to justify its existence and to enable it to continue to function. While all school curriculum and organizational patterns need to be adapted constantly to meet the ever-changing needs of the students and society, much of what is taught theoretically in college methods courses is not practical for use in the classroom. Experienced teachers have learned this discouraging fact through years of classroom experimentation resulting in both success and failure. Therefore, before the novice is overly critical and very vocal in her condemnations of the school system and the educational methods being used by her peers, she should allow herself several months in the classroom to get the "feel" of the classroom and the school situation at large. Before trying to convert the entire faculty to your point of view, you would be wise to experiment quietly on a small scale in your own classroom to see how well your theories work in practical situations. You might find that all the extra trouble you went to to construct new materials was unnecessary because your colleagues' classes learned just as much as yours following the traditional methods. If, on the other hand, you find that your new methods reaped tremendous educational successes, you might ask your department head to allow you to discuss them at a departmental meeting or you might mention what you did and how successful it was in an informal luncheon discussion or over a cup of coffee and a cigarette in the faculty room after school. Seasoned educators are usually anxious to try new techniques to add variety to their classroom activities and will be willing to listen to you if they are approached discreetly instead of being faced with a challenge and accusation of failure. Before trying to tear down the established routines of the school system in which you are employed, be certain that you have something concrete and workable to offer in return. Preview the classroom situation and teaching materials for several months before you begin to "innovate" so you know what you are trying to tear down and what foundations you wish to build upon as well as what your student potential is.

It is very easy to slip into a pattern of imposing unfairly on your colleagues and this should be avoided as much as possible. Often, several teachers have to use the same classroom facilities each day. When you find yourself in a room-sharing situation, always leave your room in good working order for any teachers who might have to use it after you. If you've been doing group work, have the students rearrange the chairs into their proper positions. Straighten the classroom facilities for the next teacher who comes in to use them. Ask your students to pick up any debris left around their desks. Erase the work you've put on the board or have one of your students erase it. Try to end your lessons when the bell rings. If your class does not leave the room promptly, the one which follows you will have to remain out in the hall and is bound to get rowdy. This will make it more difficult for their teacher to get control and begin teaching immediately. It also will take away some of the class time the teacher has planned to use for teaching her lesson.

Keep your classroom as quiet as possible. If your class is doing a "noisy" activity such as holding three or four-group discussions simultaneously or giving oral reports which might invoke class laughter, try to keep the noise at a minimum so that the classes close to you are not distracted. It might even be a good idea to send a student into the next room to ask the teacher if the noise is too loud because it is often difficult to gauge how much of your classroom sound is finding its way into adjoining rooms. This also holds true when you are showing films. The sound from film tracts travels farther than one might imagine and the entire floor might be disturbed by the movie you are showing if you are not careful.

Do not ask other teachers to excuse students from their classes to assist you or to participate in one of your activities. If a student is helping you to prepare a bulletin board for your classroom or is taking a message around to other class-rooms to obtain signatures from faculty members, do not expect another teacher to excuse him from class to help you. This is most unfair because it suggests to your colleagues that you consider your bulletin board or message to be more im-portant than what he is teaching. This is insulting as well

122

as inconsiderate because the excused student is very likely to ask his other teacher for help in making up what he missed while he was helping you. If you need a student to help you, ask him to come before or after school or during part of his lunch period. Minor subject matter teachers, such as those in physical education, art, music and cooking, are particularly sensitive about the practice of teachers asking to have students excused during their period because they meet with their pupils infrequently, often only once or twice a week, and their class time is invaluable to them. They are rightfully offended by the attitude of major subject matter teachers that they are teaching extraneous and unimportant courses which pupils can miss without incurring great educational losses.

Schools frequently have to follow a system for rotating goods and materials among the teachers of a particular department because of the shortage of such teaching aides. Department heads or book chairmen arrange intricate schedules for sharing these supplies. English teachers are often given a few weeks to use supplementary reading books with their classes before they switch them for other texts. Science and language classes are sometimes allotted only a portion of the semester during which they can make use of the science and language laboratories. It is a matter of courtesy as well as of fairness for you to finish your work with the shared materials within the amount of time you are allotted. Keeping the supplies longer than you are entitled to them disrupts another teacher's lesson plan schedule and cuts into the amount of time your colleague has to use them because she will have to relinquish them to yet another class waiting to use them. Always return books and supplies when they are due to be exchanged so that your colleagues will not have to wait or alter their lesson plans because of your inconsideration or poor planning.

There is a great deal that new teachers can learn from their older colleagues. Most experienced teachers are more than willing to share their ideas on methods for classroom control, discipline and teaching techniques if they are approached properly. If you are having troubles in any of these areas, you would be wise to go to your peers for help before turning to your department head or school principal. When you ask for suggestions, make your requests sincere ones which reflect your desire to be helpful both to yourself and to your students. Few seasoned educators can refuse requests for help.

Young teachers have a tendency to congregate with each other in the lunchroom and in the faculty room. The same thing holds true for the people who have been in the school for a long time. If you can possibly break the trend and sit with your older colleagues you can often pick up many helpful suggestions about classroom techniques as well as about how things function in the school as a whole. Every school has a system of intricacies and intrigues which rival some very exciting spy stories. Older teachers can tell you which disciplinarians and assistant vice principals are harsher in dealing with student problems, which secretaries will help you with clerical work and which book chairmen to avoid when entering requests for extra books. They can tell you how to phrase requisitions for class trips and who is more likely to grant your requests.

The seniority system in most high schools is rivaled only by that in the Congress. Teachers are awarded the smartest classes, the newest texts and the most modern equipment on the basis of the number of years they have been in the school system. As a newcomer, you can expect to have shredded books copyrighted ten years before the invention of the television, a schedule which requires you to teach four of your five classes in different classrooms, a slow class beginning at eight o'clock in the morning, and an advisory room located next to the boiler. All teachers have passed through these initiations of fire. While they can sympathize with the depression you are feeling, they do not welcome hearing about it during their lunch breaks or while they are supervising study hall with you. Therefore, while you should feel free to earnestly request advice from your more experienced colleagues do not cry and moan to them about your problems. They are there to teach and advise if they can, not offer psychiatric counseling or crying towels. Your family can provide the shoulders for moaning and you can commiserate with those who began teaching when you did and are equally depressed. Do not undermine your own self-respect by acting like a spoiled, crying child in front of your colleagues. Try to remember that after a few years, you too will have the option of selecting the grade levels you'd like to teach, the room you'd like to stay in and the textbooks you want to use.

Aside from your daily encounters with your colleagues in the halls, faculty room, dining room and while sharing supervisory duties in the halls, lavatories, study halls and lunchrooms, there will be other times when you and your colleagues are brought together. Often, department heads will suggest on the basis of your area of specialization in college, the location and size of your classroom and the needs of the student body, that you and a colleague engage in a team-teaching program. This sort of arrangement involves two or more teachers who work and plan together to present subject matter to two or more classes. The teachers involved progress with their individual classes at the same rate of speed, covering basically the same material. Their classes meet together for lectures delivered by one of the teachers in the team. This frees the other teachers to work individually with those students who need additional work of a remedial or progressive nature. The teachers lecture to the large groups on their own areas of interest and specialization. The students benefit from this type of program because they are able to hear from the best possible teachers on a given subject. The teachers benefit because they can teach what they like best about their subject matter. However, it must be remembered that this type of instruction succeeds only if all members of the team are willing to work hard at making it succeed. They must be willing to meet on their own time to plan lessons and select materials. Both teachers must be willing to contribute to their fullest potentials and not look upon team teaching as a way to avoid teaching several periods a week.

Even if you are not working on a team, it might be to your advantage to share some of your ideas with others who indicate that they will be receptive to them. Teachers are anxious to hear about techniques which have proved successful in motivating or educating pupils and will be more than willing to try them if they are suggested in a helpful rather than condescending or haughty manner. If you are anxious to bring about changes in curriculum or teaching methods on a school-wide basis, you would be wise to volunteer for membership on one of the many committees existing in each school to make suggestions for innovations and arrangements for alterations. Even as a new teacher, it should not be too difficult to gain admission to one of these communities. The principal often has difficulty finding people to man such groups and he is likely to be more than willing to find that he has some anxious volunteers on his staff.

Experienced teachers who are confident of their proficiency in the classroom are frequently willing to be observed by their younger peers. Department heads and principals will tell you which teachers are willing to be observed. Some colleagues might invite you to sit in on their classes during lunchroom conversations. You can learn a great deal about what to do and what not to do from observing people in actual practice in classroom situations which are similar to yours. Some of the things to look for in your observations and which you should try to be aware of in your own classroom are as follows:

The Classroom: What provisions are made for safety and orderliness? Are there easily accessible waste baskets? Where and how are supplies stored? Are fire and civil defense drill regulations posted in a clearly visible location? Is there adequate light and ventilation?

What indications are there of classwork being done? Are there bulletin boards and displays revealing the type and quality of work being done by the students?

Do the students display good working and study habits? Do they respect their own property and that of the school? Are they courteous to their teacher and classmates? Do they appear to be familiar with the classroom routine? Is pupil participation wide or limited to just a few pupils?

The Teacher: Does she exhibit sensitivity to each child in her room? Does she display enthusiasm for her subject matter, show courtesy, admit mistakes, move about the room gracefully, avoid excessive lecturing, accept the ideas of the children, speak too quickly, modulate her voice, show concern for the children?

The Lesson: What evidences are there of careful preplanning? Are the aims of the lesson obvious? Are all the major steps of good lesson planning included? How easily does the teacher move from one activity to another? Are visual aids being used effectively? Is the teacher trying to develop creativity and critical thinking?

Focusing your attention upon the above questions will give you some foundations upon which to evaluate the lessons you are observing and will give you some things to think about when planning and evaluating your own lesson plans.

Most teachers will be willing to answer any questions you have about their techniques as long as those questions are posed earnestly. Remember that while observing another teacher, you are a guest in that educator's classroom. Try not to exhibit any of the behavioral patterns you find disturbing in your own students such as the obvious lack of attention give-aways of staring out the window, reading a book while being lectured to, or yawning visibly or noisily.

In the secondary schools today, most faculty members belong to either a professional teachers' organization or to a union. Senior high schools seem to lean more heavily toward union membership. Before deciding which organization to join, or whether you want to join at all, try to find out what the platforms of each group are, what the dues are, and what the members receive in return for their dues. In those school systems which give teachers collective bargaining rights, you would be wise to find out which organization represents the teachers at contract negotiations and what gains they have made for the teachers in recent contract agreements.

While neither organization is likely to pressure you to join their group immediately after you sign your contract with the school system, they will try to talk you into becoming one of their members early in the semester. You can feel justified in asking for a semester or two to make up your mind. However, most teachers will find that it is to their advantage to become a member of one of the groups. The dues are reasonable and in many systems they can be deducted for you automatically from your pay checks. The teachers' organizations provide many services for their members and for non-members as well. These include representing teachers in disputes with school boards, providing additional health programs, lending money at low interest rates through credit foundations and protecting teachers against arbitrary decisions by the school board or school administration. Most union or professional association members feel that since they work ultimately to provide desirable working conditions for all faculty members that all educators in the system should support them financially by paying their dues and morally by adding their support to organizational decisions.

Virtually all school systems have dropped outmoded restrictions of teachers' social and personal lives. Years ago, smoking was cause for dismissal and female teachers were forbidden to wear skirts above their ankles or be seen out in public after eight o'clock at night. Today, urban schools permit female teachers to wear slacks to school, to teach as long as they are able to while they are pregnant, and even allow married couples to teach in the same school. It would be wise for a new teacher to discover what the social rules are from colleagues before making any major decisions. Teachers who are seeing colleagues of the opposite sex socially would be wise to be as discreet as possible. Teen-age pupils are anxious to develop any bits of scandal they can find or invent to use against a teacher who has denied to grant them a favor or has given them an unfavorable grade they feel they do not deserve. It would be wise to be as discreet as possible in your relationships with colleagues to prevent any unnecessary problems for you or your friends. Students speculate about the romantic lives of their young teachers without the least bit of encouragement. Save yourself from having to defend or explain your actions by avoiding any public relationships with colleagues which will provide factual basis for your students' gossip.

Getting along with your peers will provide many opportunities for desirable intellectual, educational and social experiences. Positive relationships with colleagues will make your working hours more pleasant and increase your effectiveness as an educator. They are something which, as a newcomer, you will have to work to achieve but good working relationships prove rewarding and beneficial to all involved.

RELATIONSHIPS WITH STUDENT TEACHERS

Shocking as this may be to the novice or potential educator, many new teachers in urban or small rural school systems find themselves in the position of having to train a student teacher while they are still learning how to teach themselves. Because of the large faculty turnover each year in city schools, there are frequently too few experienced teachers willing to take a student teacher to meet the demands of the local universities. City schools often take student teachers in return for financial aid granted to high school graduates planning to attend the universities which place the student teachers into the schools. In rural schools the beginner may be the only geometry or French teacher in the school, in which case she is the only person qualified to handle the student teachers in her subject. Fortunately for the teacher who is a novice herself, the universities usually begin their school terms a month later than the secondary schools. This gives the new teacher about a month to get herself, and her classroom, organized before her student teacher arrives. This will enable her to stay at least one step ahead of her protege, but just barely.

At the beginning of their relationship, the classroom teacher should acquaint the student teacher with school and departmental policies concerning lateness to class, procedures for checking and reporting attendance, care of books, daily lesson planning, group classifications, course aims and grading procedures.

During the period in which the student teacher is observing the professional, the latter should make every attempt to explain the rationale behind every lesson taught and the procedures used. The master teacher should attempt to make the student teacher understand her reasons for selecting each lesson she presents and the rationale behind her manner of presentation.

The professional should plan the initial lessons the student teacher will teach step by step with the student teacher to be certain that the lessons are educationally sound and that they meet the requirements of the curriculum. During the first few weeks of the student teacher's instructional experiences, the experienced educator should give the student, in writing, the good and bad points of each lesson as well as suggestions for improving the errors. After the first few weeks, the supervising teacher should begin to give weekly or biweekly written critiques of the student's performance. Copies of these brief critiques should be saved for the department head and for the student teaching supervisor. It is your responsibility to see that the student teacher does not deprive your classes of the quality of education to which they are rightfully entitled. Your first responsibilities are to your students and to the school system which hired you. Therefore, if a student teacher is not performing satisfactorily, it is your duty to report this to your department head who will either observe the student teacher himself or will contact the student teaching supervisor and ask her to check on the student's progress.

The classroom teacher should check the daily lesson plans of her student teacher at least three days before the student intends to teach the lesson. She should make certain that the aims, methods and materials meet the needs of the grade levels to be taught. Encourage the student teacher to enforce school policies and regulations the way you would if you were in charge. Check her records of attendance and grades to be certain that they are accurate and up-to-date. It is to your advantage to keep a copy of all grades she gives so that when she leaves at the end of her term you will not be left with an empty mark book. Before the student teacher returns homework or test papers she has graded, review the papers to see that she was not too lenient, careless or demanding in her grading.

As you are the professional, the students will often look to you for decisions and information rather than to the student teacher because they know that the student is just that, another student, and that you are the ultimate authority. Do not fall into the trap of interfering between the student teacher and the pupils unless it is absolutely necessary to do so. Once you undermine her authority by contradicting her or countermanding her orders in front of the class, she will never be able to regain their respect or maintain classroom control. Tell the students to speak directly to the student teacher about any problems or questions they may have. Refraining from interrupting lessons to express your point of view will require the exercise of much self-restraint, but it is a sacrifice you owe to your student teacher.

Many educators look upon having a student teacher as receiving a vacation from the classroom. This should not be the case. The professional teacher should never leave the student teacher alone in the room with the class. Students, seeing the professional leaving the room, think they have been given a great opportunity to test the strength of the student teacher and have a good time in the process. Should personal injury or property damage occur in your absence, the school system will hold you responsible. The extra cup of coffee or cigarette you have while you are out of the room is not worth the chance you take by leaving an inexperienced student alone with your class.

Taking on the responsibility of training a student teacher is both time-consuming and rewarding. While the teacher must surrender some of her free periods, her lunch periods or stay after school to work with the student teacher, she is given the unique opportunity of being able to teach in a double capacity—that of classroom teacher and that of teacher-trainer. Student teachers are generally very sensitive people because they are in a very tenuous position. They are serving in the roles of teachers, and have the responsibilities of teachers, yet they don't have the punitive rights or the authority of the professionals. They function in the roles of teachers, yet they are students themselves. The professional who works with a student teacher must proceed with great tact and caution, especially if she is insecure and inexperienced herself. Many potentially good teachers are lost as a result of unsatisfactory student teaching experiences. Therefore, the professional who can establish a good working relationship with her student teacher is performing a service not only to herself and the student teacher but to the school district and future students as well.

RELATIONSHIPS WITH PRINCIPALS AND OTHER ADMINISTRATORS

In large urban school systems, unless the novice finds herself saddled with an important committee assignment or sponsorship of a major student activity such as the newspaper or yearbook, she rarely meets with the principal on an individual basis after their initial introductions except for brief and impersonal encounters at faculty affairs at Christmas, Easter and the end of the semester. Principals are too busy to handle the daily problems which arise in individual classrooms. The liaison person between the classroom teacher and the principal and administrators of the school district is the chairman or department head of each individual subject matter area. It is through him that the teacher must go if she wishes to get extra supplies, have severe discipline problems handled, gain opportunities to serve on committees, be appointed to sponsor extra-curricular activities and get information about supplementary jobs with the school system from which teachers can gain extra money and experience. If your department head cannot arrange these things for you, he can put you in touch with the people who can.

The first person who will give you more than a general introduction to your particular school situation is the chairman of your department. He will tell you the specific information you need to know about your teaching duties. He will tell you when you are expected to report for school in the morning, where your classes meet, what the ability level indicators of your classes mean, what texts you will be using, what the dress regulations for teachers and students are, how and to whom you report excused absences from school or from your class and how to record attendance daily. If you are given your teaching assignment more than a few hours before you are to begin teaching, try to contact your department head to find out what grade levels and texts you will have to deal with in your new assignment. He will be pleased to give you copies of these books so you can begin to read them immediately. As a new teacher, you'll have enough to do during your first few weeks without having to read as many as five different textbooks before you start planning lessons related to them. The earlier you know what books you are using and begin studying them, the fewer pressures you'll have to cope with when the school semester starts.

Many chairmen will try to keep a check on the activities of the novice by requiring her to turn in detailed lesson plans one week in advance of the time they are to be taught for the first six months to a year that she is in the school. He is

133

justified in this demand. School principals hold him responsible for knowing about the classroom activities and competence of the teachers in his department. Complaints and questions about what is going on in your room will be directed to him for investigation. For the benefit of the students, the school system and the teacher herself, it is important that the department head keep himself well informed about classroom procedures. Supervision of lesson plans should be viewed as an attempt to prevent potential problems rather than a spying or prying tactic.

After your first few conferences with your department head, you would be wise to avoid any unnecessary contact with him. Coming to him with complaints or problems you cannot handle will make him suspicious about your competency and he is likely to watch you so carefully that you will feel stifled and he will be aware of every minor mistake you make. Save your visits for important problems and try to handle the minor ones yourself.

Teachers receive ratings periodically which are used in granting tenure and promotions. These ratings are assigned primarily on the basis of observations made by the department chairman or the principals themselves. It is very common to become nervous and flustered when an outsider, particularly one who is there to observe and assign a grade, is present in the classroom. It seems as though the department head always selects the day you got to school late or the day twenty of your students forget to bring their textbooks to class to make an impromptu visit to your room. To prevent this from happening, the new teacher would be wise to send an invitation to the principal or department head asking him to attend her class on a selected day during a particular period when she plans to present a lesson which she hopes will be particularly effective. It would be wise to list one or two alternate dates in case the first one is not practical for the observer. Most administrators will be willing to oblige by making every effort to comply with your request.

Another way to let the administration know how successfully you are functioning in the classroom is to send them interesting samples of your student's work. This does not mean that you deluge their mailboxes with test papers which have been graded "A," but it does mean that if your classes put together a booklet they have written or constructed unusual geometric models, samples of their work could be placed in your superior's mailboxes or posted on clearly-visible hallway bulletin boards.

Volunteering to help with unpleasant duties such as arranging for the clean-up after the senior prom or staying late to tutor slow students when there is no additional financial compensation involved are ways of making the administration aware of your dedication. You will want them to know this if you hope that they will recommend you for summer school teaching appointments, promotions or popular extracurricular duties for which there is frequently extra financial compensation such as a newspaper sponsor or dramatic club coach.

While it has been suggested that the classroom teacher should not run to administrators with every classroom problem she encounters, it is not to be assumed that the teacher should not consult her superiors for help in dealing with individual problems with which they might have more experience or be more qualified to handle. For example, if you discover that one of your students is seriously emotionally disturbed or in great financial need, your department head or principal is more qualified to find help for this student than you are and they will tell you how to handle the problem or will handle it for you. On the other hand, you should not expect them to punish a student who repeatedly comes to your class late or who is inattentive while you are trying to teach. These are things which administrators are reasonable in expecting you to handle for yourself. If every teacher reported all her minor problems to the department head, the department chairman would spend his entire day handling minor discipline cases the teacher should be able to handle herself.

One of the most disappointing revelations on entering the teaching profession is the discovery that very little occurs at faculty and departmental meetings. High school students imagine that all sorts of exciting, secretive plots are concocted by faculty members at their meetings to make them emerge victorious over the student body. Your first encounter with a faculty meeting is very likely to be disappointing. These gatherings are usually scheduled because the school board requires principals and department heads to meet with the staff periodically. These meetings are routine and the material given to you by the leader could well be rex-o-graphed and put into faculty mailboxes. Depending upon the character of your school principal, the meetings could be enjoyable or deadly. If the principal is aware of his faculty's feelings about attending meetings at the end of the school day when they are tired, or returning at night when they'd rather be with their families or arriving early in the morning before they are fully awake and if he agrees with them, he will make his meetings as short and enjoyable as possible. Other administrators who feel the need to exert their power or enjoy seeing their subjects seated before them will talk as long as they possibly can on as many subjects as they possibly can. Whichever type of principal you have, faculty meetings are a reality of the educational program which have to be accepted. The greatest contribution of such meetings lies in the fact that they give you an opportunity to meet with faculty members you don't get a chance to see in the normal course of the school schedule and that they give you an opportunity to hear how you sound to your students when they are tired and you are over-using the lecture method of teaching.

In order to establish a satisfactory working relationship with administrators who can be vital in determining whether your experiences in your school are pleasurable or unsatisfactory, you must bear in mind what goals the principal and department chairman hope to accomplish. What they want is to have a smooth-running school with as few problems as possible with optimum learning occurring. Therefore, a good rule to follow in your relationship with your supervisors is to bother them as infrequently as possible with your problems and to send them frequent reports on your successes. This will help them to remember your name above the other two to three hundred teachers found in many urban secondary schools and they will think of you in connection with promotions and high ratings.

RELATIONSHIPS WITH PARENTS

Pediatricians report that the biggest problems they have in their practices result not from coping with illness or from dealing with their young patients, but from communicating with their patients' parents. The school teacher can readily empathize with the physician's plight. Often the teacher's biggest problems come from trying to get along with angry, concerned or irate parents. Yet, parents could be a great source of help to the teacher by giving additional assistance at home to students at both ends of the achievement spectrum. They can be invaluable sources of information in helping teachers cope with discipline and emotional problems. They can be of service to the school by working through the P.T.A. to gather funds for equipment and can help individually by accompanying teachers on trips to supervise pupils and assist at sporting and social events. In large city schools, the majority of the faculty members often do not have direct contact with the P.T.A. Several volunteers are selected from the faculty to represent their colleagues at meetings, although the meetings are opened to any faculty member who wishes to participate.

The most direct contact that the classroom teacher will have with groups of parents will occur at parent-teacher meetings usually scheduled shortly after the opening of school and after each report card has been distributed. At the opening of each of these meetings, the teacher should speak to the parents as a group about the work the class has been doing, what her standards of achievement are and what she hopes they will accomplish as the term progresses. This will make repetition of the same information unnecessary. Then she can answer questions from the group and finally proceed to personal discussions with parents about their individual children. When preparing these encounters with parents, the teacher would be wise to have her grade book up to date and to display samples of her pupils' work clearly throughout the classroom. Some schools invite parents to open houses at which time they can observe the teacher conducting a class. At this time the teacher might ask parents to attend future events such as debates or speeches and to go along on trips to help the teacher supervise the class. Experienced teachers will attest to the fact that the parents of problem children whom they particularly want to meet rarely appear at these events and have to be sent for.

As problems arise during the term, the teacher should feel free to contact individual parents personally. If a student is consistently doing failing work or is cutting classes, the teacher should inform the parents of this as soon as possible. This will remove her from any possible castigation when, after report grades are given out, the parents come to the school and complain "Why weren't we informed? We didn't know anything about it." Some schools have form letters which can be sent to parents informing them of their children's deficiency in scholarship or problems in behavior. In some schools, the proper procedure for handling parent-teacher contacts is to report problems to the counseling office which will then arrange an appointment for the parent with the teacher. Before contacting a parent personally, check with a colleague or a department head to see what procedures your school follows.

Teachers find that the problems of dealing with parents who are totally detached and who don't care whether their children set fires in the lavatories or drop textbooks out of windows are as great as those incurred while coping with parents who are overly-involved with their children. This latter type of parent is often one who was a teacher himself or who has a cousin who was a teacher who knows a much better way to teach the "new math" than you do and who can't understand why the English teacher has assigned so controversial a book as *Catcher in the Rye*. The teacher should try to remember that this type of parent has good intentions and is proceeding under what he feels are the best interests of his children. The only recourse the teacher has is to smile through her clenched teeth and remember that the school term only lasts ten months. Hopefully, in a dispute between a parent and a teacher, the department head or principal will support the teacher. The majority can be counted upon to do this. If they do not, you will have to re-examine the situation to determine whether the attitude of your deparment head is too inhibiting for you as an educator. If it is, you will have to seek employment elsewhere. If, however, all the other teaching conditions in the school are desirable you will have to try to overlook this difficulty and drink a little extra milk to calm your ulcer.

In many ghetto areas, it is virtually impossible to get parents to come to school to discuss their children's learning or adjustment difficulties. This is due in some cases to a distrust of the school as an alien influence. In some cases this is due to a lack of parental concern and in other instances to the fact that working parents cannot afford to take time from their jobs or find people to care for the young children still at home while they go to school to meet with teachers. In situations such as these, with the consent of the school administration, it is a good idea for the classroom teacher to visit the homes of some of her problem pupils. This can be done after school or, if the parents are employed, the visits can be made in the evening.

The teacher should not plan to go on ventures such as these without the prior consent of her department head or school principal. Often, these people can alert you to parents who are likely to be offensive or belligerent. The teacher should not make these visits alone. Pairs of educators, preferably male-female teams should work together. The prevailing attitude for these visits should reflect the instructor's sincere desire to bring the school and the home closer together for the purpose of helping the student to reach his full potential—not one of accusation suggesting that the home has failed the pupil or that parental interest has been inadequate. Again, it cannot be stressed too strongly that visits of this type should only be attempted after the school administration has been consulted. Some school districts employ community-relations personnel who will assist you in planning these meetings.

If home visitations are impractical because of community resentment, potential danger to the teacher's physical well-being or lack of time, each new teacher owes it to herself and her pupils to arrange to take a walking or driving tour of the area served by the school in which she is employed. Viewing the types of homes from which her pupils come and the environment in which they are living will give the teacher an added insight into the problems with which her students must cope and might even open the educator's eyes to conditions with which she had never before come in contact.

RELATIONSHIPS WITH STUDENTS

Ultimately, the most important people the teacher must get along with are her students. The relationship between teacher and student has changed radically in the last decade. In the "olden times" teachers were revered by students. Teachers seemed to exist in vacuums of perfection, taken out of glass cases in the morning and put back in immediately after the school day ended. Students giggled quietly when, if by accident, they saw their teachers in a movie theater or stared, with mouths agape, if they met them in such undignified places as supermarkets and bowling alleys. Today things are different. Students expect their teachers to "be with it." They want their educators to "rap" with them on the issues of the time. Many schools now permit their female teachers to come to school dressed in slacks and men wear mod clothes. In an era in which students demand that they be given a voice in curriculum planning and making school policy decisions, teachers walk a very thin line between undermining their authority by being too friendly and alienating their classes by being "irrelevant" and aloof.

One of the things young people of today are demanding in their relationships with adults is honesty. Do not try to be something that you are not. If your personality is one that recoils at the idea of being a strong authoritarian or dictatorial figure, do not try to be one in the classroom. If a student says something which is funny, laugh. If you are angry, show your anger. If you have made a mistake in a decision or in some information given to the class, admit your error. Do not compound your poor judgment by enforcing a bad rule or assignment just because you made the rule and are ashamed to confess your mistake. If you do not know the answer to a question, tell the students that you do not know but that you will find the answer for them. If you tell them that you will find information for them, be certain that you do so. Write a reminder for yourself so that you don't forget. If you don't bring the information to the next class meeting, students will suspect that you were just putting them off with your promise and that you never intended to find the information in the first place.

Do not break any promises that you make to a class or individual pupil. If you promise to bring in a book for supplementary reading, help a student after school or write a letter of recommendation for a college or job, be certain that you keep those vows. If the students cannot believe what you tell them of a personal nature, how can they believe what you say about your subject matter or its relevancy to them? If you offer the class a reward for work well done or threaten them with punishment for unsatisfactory behavior be certain to carry out what you have promised. For this reason, it is important that you are certain before you make any promises that you can carry out what you have suggested.

Students rate fairness as a high priority characteristic for a teacher to possess. Avoid selecting favorite students. Repeatedly calling on the same pupils to do favors for you and answer questions gives rise to unpleasant feelings toward both you and the pupils involved. Treat all students with equal harshness or leniency.

Do not mete out excessive punishment or punish the entire class for the actions of a few. It is often wiser to ignore or overlook the misbehavior if you cannot select the troublemakers than it is to alienate an entire class by punishing the innocent along with the guilty. Do not allow anger to goad you into giving excessively harsh punishments. A week of detentions is unreasonably severe for the first offense of cracking chewing gum in class or sneezing loudly to gain attention, but it is not too harsh for repeated instances of misbehavior such as unexcused absences from class and failures to do assigned work.

While the teacher should exhibit warmth and an honest concern for the welfare of her pupils, she must be extremely careful not to become too friendly or too involved with her pupils. Compromising situations should be avoided. There are many teen-agers of sixteen and seventeen years who are men and women, not children. There are also teen-agers in the junior high schools of thirteen and fourteen years who think they are men and women. Therefore, teachers must be extremely careful in their relationships with students of the opposite sex. Never allow yourself to be alone with a student of the opposite sex. If you have to punish a student by keeping him in after school or give him extra help, find some excuse to detain another student to help you cover a set of books or decorate a bulletin board. If this is not practical, take the lone student to a more public place than your classroom such as the department head's office or counseling offices where there are other people in nearby cubicles. Spurned or angry students can raise some very nasty suspicions about a teacher which, even when proven false, will hang over the teacher's entire career and cloud her reputation in the school and in the community. Should a student express honest affection for a teacher, the educator should try to handle the expression of devotion as tactfully as possible. Laughing it off will only embarrass the pupil and set up a wall through which it will be almost impossible to educate. The best advice is to try to prevent such admissions of affection from occurring. If you sense that a student is about to express his love for you, try to change the subject to avoid embarrassment for both of you.

While a teacher should express a sincere interest in the concerns of her pupils, she should avoid encouraging confidences. A teacher can be placed in a very awkward position if she allows pupils to confide information of a personal or illegal nature to her. Being in the position of knowing that one of your young female students intends to obtain an illegal abortion over the weekend or that one of your brightest boys is using drugs poses a very difficult problem. Betraying a confidence is deadly to the positive relationship which caused it to occur in the first place. Not revealing what you know may be contrary to the student's best interest and possibly even against the law. Therefore, you should always warn a student who wishes to tell you something of a personal nature that you will be more than willing to help him but that you cannot guarantee to keep what he tells you a secret. It is very difficult for a teacher to sleep at night knowing that she is the only one who knows that the students are planning to burn the Record's Office in the morning and keep the gym teacher as hostage in return for amnesty for four pupils suspended for smoking marijuana at the senior prom. Along with all the other problems a new teacher has, do not take on the added problem of wrestling with your conscience into the middle of a sleepless night. You need that time to grade papers and plan lessons. Never agree to keep a confidence a secret until after you have heard it. Forewarn pupils that you will act upon what they tell you in a manner beneficial to all concerned.

In addition to educating pupils, the classroom teacher is responsible for protecting their physical safety and well-being. Students, who because of their emotional or social instability threaten the rest of the class, should be removed from the classroom as soon as possible. Teachers should report incidents of pupils who carry dangerous weapons such as knives, guns and brass knuckles to the department head or person in charge of discipline. Do not engage in heroics by demanding that the student turn the weapon over to you or by trying to disarm him. You are not only placing yourself in danger if you do so, but you are taking serious chances with the welfare of your entire class.

Urban high schools frequently harbor within their student bodies card-carrying, zip-gun packing, penknife-toting members of rival gangs. You can easily learn the names of the gangs functioning within the district served by your schools by checking the names scrawled on the walls, desks and textbooks. As a classroom teacher, you would be wise to learn as much as you can about your pupils' gang affiliations without prying or appearing to delve into matters which the students think do not concern you. One of the safest ways to learn who travels with which group is to be aware of the names your students have tattooed on their arms, hands and foreheads. Notice also the colors of your students' jackets and beanies. These items reflect the clubs' colors and often have the student's name and their gang affiliations imprinted somewhere on them. Aside from satisfying the teacher's curiosity, knowing about students' loyalties can do much to offset difficulties in the classroom by preventing you from making unfortunate combinations. For example, matching the warlord of the Red Hatters with the triggerman for the Singing Dolphins for a class project could literally prove to be deadly.

It cannot be stressed too strongly, however, that although the teacher should make every discreet endeavor possible to

144

know as much as she can about her students' outside interests, both legal and illegal, she should never try to interfere with these activities. One classroom teacher, no matter how popular, trusted or well liked, cannot make peace between rival gang factions who have been at war for years before she became associated with the school system. Remember that you are a trained educator, not a trained gang control worker. The most that you can hope to do through your knowledge of gang activities and affiliations is to try to avoid trouble caused by unwise grouping arrangements and possibly to alert officials to potential future trouble. Do not expect students to tell you who "heisted" the principal's car or who messed up the kid found walking unescorted through rival turf. No matter how favorably students react to you, they will never welcome you into the inner sanctum of their gang activities. This is probably much to your benefit since the knowledge of their exploits might be more than you will want to bear.

Mass student action, such as taking over administrative offices or holding sit-down and sit-in strikes, is very common today and the new teacher should be prepared psychologically to face such events when they occur in her classroom or in the school as a whole. Should the action of the students involve the entire school population, there is nothing the individual teacher can do. Decisions, relationships with the students and negotiations will be handled by the administration. However, if the action takes place in your classroom alone, judge the mood of the crowd before taking any action. If the students are basically jovial or calm, you might try to reason with them and agree to discuss any problems with a few of their chosen representatives. If the crowd has turned into an ugly mob, there is no point in trying to reason with them. Try to stay away from them while sending for more qualified and numerous help and doing whatever can reasonably be done to prevent them from bringing harm to themselves or to others.

In the event of mass student rebellion, the teacher must remember that she is not "super educator" and she should

145

not attempt to handle more than any single human being is reasonably expected to cope with. You alone cannot calm an entire hallway of demonstrating students. There are security personnel accessible to the administration who will be called to control the situation if the need arises. Placing yourself in the middle of the demonstration could further aggravate the problems by infuriating students who do not recognize your desire to help or by arousing passions on both sides when you are accidentally pushed, shoved or injured. Likewise, you should not try to physically restrain pupils who are attempting to leave the school or your classroom to join a demonstration or protest. You would be wiser to let them join their comrades without interference and decide what action, if any, to take after quiet, calm speculation and consultation with administrative personnel. Despite the fact that it may seem undignified and insulting to simply step back and allow students to run out of your classroom to join a demonstration taking place in the hall or street without your permission, you must admit that you will not be any more dignified lying flat on your back staring up at the students who have stepped on you on their way out the door.

One major decision an educator is likely to be faced with in this era of student activism is that of whether or not to join students in their protest movements. It is impossible here to give a hard and fast rule which will cover all types of demonstrations. Student protests range from such harmless protests as girls wearing their gym bloomers backwards in protest against outmoded dress codes and boys eating their lunches in the school yard to show their desire for coeducational eating facilities to burning and rioting over curriculum changes and alleged infringements upon student freedoms. You will have to judge each situation individually to determine if it is important enough to warrant your taking a chance on losing your teaching position. If it is, then you should lend your more mature judgment and direction to the student activity. To refrain from doing so would seriously damage your own self-respect and render you ineffectual in the classroom.

However, if you are not certain that you are deeply committed to the same ends as the students, do not engage in demonstrations just to be popular. As a novice to the school you might be wise to refrain from participating until you know what the school situation is. Whether you decide to participate or not, the most important thought in your mind should be protecting the physical and emotional safety of both those students who are participating in the action and those who are not.

A teacher can make a major contribution to the students' emotional well-being by indicating that she understands their needs. This can be done in discussions involving subject matter as well as in personal conversations. When you talk to your pupils indicate that you have not only heard what they have said but that you were listening to what they said. For example, when a student tells you in answer to a question that the "Southern states were crazy to secede from the Union" you might phrase your reply to him in the following manner: "John, then you think the confederacy made an error in judgment. Why?" This indicates that you heard and understood his point of view and are interested in really listening to what he has to say. This technique of reflecting your understanding of the pupil's point of view encourages him to continue to express himself because he knows that you care. This technique can be used in personal situations also. When a student confronts you with a statement like, "You hate me. You always pick on me," the student is obviously overwrought and upset. He is more likely to hear you when you reflect his feelings by saying, "You think I haven't treated you fairly? Let's see what makes you feel this way," than he is if you dismiss him by saying, "That's silly. I never pick on students."

Try to keep the word "I" out of your conversation as much as you possibly can. Instead, substitute the word "You," as in " 'You' will need to know how to use equations to solve for unknowns," as opposed to " 'I' want you to learn how to use equations" or " 'You' will be able to see the board more easily if you face the front of the room rather than the back," instead of, " 'I' insist that you turn around immediately and face the front of the room." This will make you appear less dictatorial in your decisions and more concerned with your pupils' needs.

Coping with racial problems is difficult on a nationwide scale so it is understandable that it would be difficult to handle them in schools and in individual classrooms. With increased bussing and reshaping of school boundaries to foster integration occurring in many school districts against the expressed wishes of some of the students' parents, the new teacher is bound to encounter some racial problems during her early years of teaching. It is important to be realistic and realize that you cannot reverse twelve to seventeen years of prejudice and bigotry during your 45-minute class periods. However, you can make small contributions to understanding and communication through pairing partners of different racial backgrounds for group projects. Teachers of the social sciences have increased opportunities for trying to improve racial harmony through the use of selected materials and research projects. While you cannot hope to make pupils love their classmates of different racial origins, if you can bring about some understanding you will have made a worthy contribution to their social development and to society as a whole.

To insure your own emotional and physical well-being, there are several don'ts you should bear in mind in your relationship with your students. Never turn your back on a class. Even if you are writing on the board, practice the technique of looking over your right shoulder as you write if you are right-handed or over the left if you are left-handed. This will prevent students from throwing things such as books, lunches and chairs at you and at each other while your vision is obstructed. Second, never let a class see you cry. Once a class has made you cry, you will have no peace. They will try to torment you every chance they get. It also follows that you should never beg or plead with a class to cooperate with you. If you lower yourself in their eyes, you will also lower yourself in your own eyes and will have to work doubly hard to regain their respect and cooperation. Third, never allow students to put you in the position of joining in or listening to gossip or complaints about another teacher. It is unprofessional to discuss or criticize another faculty member or administrator. Your feelings about your colleagues can be shared with your peers but not with your students.

EXTRACURRICULAR ACTIVITIES

Teachers frequently have duties assigned outside of those which involve actual teaching in the classroom. These chores are of four types: supervisory, compulsory club sponsorship, optional activity sponsorship, and affair attendance. The first category includes those chores which are part of the normal school roster. They include working on roster preparation, supervising the lunchrooms, study halls, libraries, lavatories and school yards, standing at the top of steep flights of stairs directing traffic and tempting would-be shovers, running the book rooms and serving in the college guidance offices. Since almost every teacher in the school will assume one of these duties for several periods each week, the new teacher would be wise to look around at possible duties, see which repel her and offend her sense of dignity the least and then file a formal request with the person in charge that she be given one of those duties she prefers in her second year. As a newcomer you really don't have much of a choice and you'll have to take what you are given. In some progressive school districts supervisory chores are being taken over by paid nonteaching assistants who are often retired policeman or ex-karate champions. Such personnel are infinitely more qualified to supervise lunchrooms and study halls than a twenty-one year old 111 pound graduate of an all-female university who majored in Chaucer and minored in education.

Another type of duty of which a teacher is not given a choice is that of being an advisor. Some schools call the period in the morning when roll is taken and announcements are read "homeroom" and some call it "advisory." Whatever it is called, it is one of the major reasons teachers begin their days in bad frames of mind. Advisory sections are notoriously difficult to control because the students know that the grades they receive, if they receive any grades at all, only reflect their cooperation or more likely, their lack of it. It is also a time during which groups such as the student council and the newspaper and yearbook staffs meet to organize their activities. This presents quite a problem for the advisor because during this period she is expected to check the daily attendance, collect money for class dues and fund raising drives, conduct elections, sell tickets, distribute lockers, read announcements, handle course selections for the next term and, if any time remains, help students with the problems they are having in their schoolwork. While you will be extremely busy during this time period trying to remember everything you have to do and attempting to do it, your students will have relatively little to keep them occupied. They will be very bored and disinterested. Idle students can always be counted on to find things to interest them such as burning the teacher in effigy, starting dice games in the back of the room or trying to "hook" their peers on pot. They also try to roam around the room aimlessly looking for more excitement than there is in their corner of the room. This is an impossible situation to allow to exist. Not only is it potentially dangerous for the pupils and teachers, but it makes performing the necessary homeroom chores mentioned above impossible. The most important of these duties is checking attendance.

Attendance must be checked daily. This is not only a school district policy but is a legal requirement. Schools traditionally divide their students alphabetically at each grade level and divide them into groups of between thirty and forty pupils. Almost every teacher in the school receives one of these groups. The pupils report to their assigned homerooms every morning before classes begin. Each advisor is given a roll book which has one roll sheet for each pupil and which is kept in a central location in the administrative offices. As she enters the building each morning the teacher should pick up the book and take it to class with her. After advisory, she can either return the book to the office herself or select a responsible student to do it for her. The individual roll sheets have the pupil's name, address, phone number, birthdate, guardian's name and number of absences last year recorded on them. In addition to the advisor's other duties, she must check the roll sheet information periodically to be certain that it is current. The roll sheets have blocks for each school day in which you record the pupil's attendance or lack of it. Most districts prefer that you write nothing in the block if the student is present, an "A" if the student is absent and an "X" if he reports to school late. When the student brings a note from his parents explaining the reason for his absence, it can be recorded by circling the "A" or putting a diagonal line through it. Students who have many absences should be reported to the school counselor or attendance officer who will check the record to decide if further investigation is necessary. When a teacher notices that a student is frequently absent, she would be wise to check the number of absences the pupil had last year to see if a previous pattern of truancy or nonattendance is indicated. The record of previous attendance patterns might alert the teacher to possible future attendance problems.

Checking attendance is one of the homeroom teacher's most important functions. This is because in checking attendance, the educator is complying with state laws as well as with school regulations. It is vital that the attendance records be accurate for several reasons. First, funds are awarded to school districts on the basis of the number of students they have in the classroom. Your records are used in compiling these figures. Second, your records might be checked in legal cases involving truancy and more serious crimes. Third, on the basis of your reports, most secondary schools publish daily lists of absentees which are distributed to the entire faculty. The faculty members use these lists after they have taken roll in their individual rooms to see which students were absent from school and which were cutting classes. If you have marked a present student absent, he can cut whichever classes he wishes without fear of reprisals. If the reverse has occurred, the absent student whose name does not appear on the list will be reported by all his subject matter teachers for being illegally absent from class.

Because checking attendance is so important, the homeroom teacher should insist upon being seen personally by every student in her section before they go to other rooms. Since advisory is universally accepted as the appropriate time to see one's counselor, return a book to the library, see another teacher about a missed assignment, go to the nurse, or any other of the very inventive excuses students offer for leaving the room, you will find that you have more empty seats than occupied ones. If you are not strict about students remaining in the room, you will find scraps of paper on the table indicating "Mary went to the library." Names and places will be scribbled on the board in the manner of "John Smith—bathroom, Carol Snyder—banking office," and you will receive third-hand oral messages such as "Steven told Carol to tell me to tell you that he had to go to a soap-carving club organizational meeting." These messages will often reach you about five minutes after you have sent the absentee list to the office. Therefore, insisting that all your advisees be physically present and in their assigned seats until the roll has been checked will make things easier for you and your pupils.

Since there are so many chores which must be accomplished during advisory period, the homeroom teacher would be wise to insist that all pupils be occupied with a quiet activity such as studying or reading the morning paper. If students object with "I did my homework already," the teacher has a valid recourse in the statement that any student who has all A's on his report card does not have to study. The rest all have something they can review or preview. For the infinitely small number of students who fit into the all-A category you can make an exception. Since they are very unlikely to present behavior problems, you don't have to worry about them. For the few students who insist they have nothing to do, bring in some old magazines which you can give them to read silently.

Collecting money for school events and charity drives is another time-consuming and difficult chore the advisor must conduct or supervise. Since money is easily lost or stolen, it would be best for the teacher to handle all collections herself. If this is not feasible, a very reliable student should be appointed, not elected, to handle the job. Money collections should be handled with the least possible confusion. Have one student approach the desk of a collector at a time. Do not allow a mob to congregate around a desk. The anonymity of a mob encourages the strange disappearance of money. Once the money has been collected, do not tempt would-be thieves by keeping the money in a desk drawer or carrying it around with you. Take it to the main office and have it placed in the school vault for safe keeping until the charity drive or event is over and all the money can be turned in at once. Always remind pupils well in advance of a money collection to give those who are short of funds an opportunity to save some money. Never pressure a student into contributing to a charity drive or buying a ticket to a school event just to insure a class of achieving 100%. He will rightfully resent you for doing this. If the class is very close to achieving 100% participation and is working for a reward, you might speak to the hold-outs individually to determine if they can afford to participate and to ask them to make every effort to chip in. They will be under enough pressure from their classmates to join in so you can remain free of the stigma of making the student feel uncomfortable.

Some schools require teachers to attend and chaperone student affairs such as proms, plays and football games. Others make it optional. It is a good idea for the classroom teacher to attend these events as frequently as she possibly can. Aside from the obvious benefit of showing the pupils that she is interested in them, other positive results can be gained also. Teachers and pupils can gain new insights into each others' personalities and talents. A teacher might see a student acting in a play or participating in a gymnastic event who refuses to read a book or do research reports. Knowing something about your students' extracurricular interests will enable you to suggest outside work for them to do. Students who see you exhibiting an interest in their concerns are more likely to react favorably to you. Therefore, all parties reap gains from attendance at these affairs aside from the most obvious one, having an enjoyable evening.

In junior high schools, or middle schools as the grades 7-9 are called in some areas, club sponsorship is almost compulsory. Club periods are rostered into the students' schedules once or twice a week. They range from such non-time-consuming activities as sponsoring the soap carving club, the aluminum foil sculpturing group and the stamp collecting society to those involving much preparation such as publishing the newspaper and sponsoring student government groups. Most schools in which club sponsorship once or twice a week is a requirement for all teachers grant a great deal of leeway to the individual teachers to lead groups which satisfy their own interests. A teacher can organize a folk music club, a sketching club, a model car building club, or any type of club which reflects the personal interests of the educator. The new teacher would be wise to head a club which involves little physical activity, no collection of money or supplies and as little confusion as possible. Stamp trading, model car building and paper flower making are examples of this type of activity in which the student brings his own materials and works individually without too much instruction or preparation for the teacher.

In the senior high schools, teachers are usually given a choice about sponsoring clubs. Few teachers are ever forced into sponsoring groups and many urban systems compensate teachers financially or with shorter teaching schedules for supervising very demanding and time-consuming activities such as the football and basketball teams, school newspaper, yearbook, dramatics club, chorus, student government and senior and junior class activities. These activities demand a lot of knowledge and preparation. The new teacher would be wise to avoid such activities for at least the first few years. Few administrators will try to force a new teacher into accepting so great a responsibility. Whether you decide to sponsor any group of students is, of course, a matter of individual taste and the amount of free time you have available to devote to after-school activities. Should you decide to sponsor one of the minor groups or a major activity in the future, you will find that, as with attending school affairs, the rewards are great. Sponsoring student groups is one of the few opportunities the classroom teacher in a large school district has to get to know any of her pupils on a personal basis. Communicating with students in an informal situation helps to keep the teacher aware of the ever-changing interests of youth and enables her to "keep with it" in her lesson planning and in her personal points of view. Be certain that you remember the basic rules stressed earlier about handling students in personal and individual situations. Never be alone with a member of the opposite sex. Do not allow students, especially girls, to work so late with you on a project at school that they have to go home alone in the dark. And do not take students on trips away from the school building without first securing written permission from their parents and from school authorities.

RELATIONSHIPS WITH SUPPORTIVE PERSONNEL

Lay Readers: Some more affluent school districts hire part-time personnel to help teachers read and grade papers. These people are professionals who are retired, on maternity leave or who only want to work a few hours a week for a variety of personal reasons. They have experience in teaching your subject matter or have majored in it in college. It would be wise for you to invite your lay reader to attend some of your classes to see how you present your material to your classes. The reader should also be given a check list of things to look for in the papers and several samples of papers you have graded so that she will know how you want your class work evaluated. Until you are confident that the lay reader's grading standards reflect your requirements, always review graded papers before returning them to the students in order to be certain that you agree with the reader's evaluation. Ultimately, you are responsible for all assigned grades and must be prepared to defend all the marks your pupils receive.

School Secretaries: School secretaries are firmly convinced, contrary to what most teachers believe, that they are the cornerstones of the educational hierarchy and that without their guidance and supervision, the teachers would cause the system to collapse in shambles. They are reluctant to allow teachers to use the rex-o-graph machines and have tantrums when teachers fail to turn reports and forms in exactly when they are due. The new teacher would be wise to play along with the secretaries in their feelings of grandeur. The secretarial staff can do much to make the educator's day more pleasant or to turn it into one of constant annoyances with messages, forms to be filled out, irritating phone calls about social security numbers in the middle of the class and refusals to give out school stationery for professional letters. On the other hand, the secretaries can do little favors for the educator such as finding needed supplies in a pinch, not reporting them for forgetting to sign in in the morning, arranging for them to see the principal without waiting for a week, and even typing stencils for them in special situations. Humoring the secretaries' delusions of grandeur and possibly even bringing them a box of cookies at Christmas will make the teaching day a little more pleasant for the teacher.

Custodial Staff: The people who clean and maintain classrooms are usually underpaid and underrespected. Students leave chewing gum on desks, paper on floors, dead frogs in waste baskets and graffiti on walls. Custodians are expected to clean all this trash cheerfully day after day without any recognition. The classroom teacher would be both wise and humane to try to establish a good relationship with the people who clean her room by thanking them occasionally for the job they do, by seeing to it that her students straighten the room as much as possible before they leave it and by remembering them at Christmas with small gifts such as dusting powder and after-shave lotion. These people are very influential in getting your torn window shades repaired, pencil sharpeners sharpened and broken desks mended. Your courtesies to them will not only be greatly appreciated but will be rewarded by little favors that you cannot imagine you will need until you begin teaching. Maintenance personnel who are on your side will be less likely to tell your supervisors and colleagues about the smoldering erasers your rapid class hid in the light fixture, the wads of chewing gum your slow class threw up to the ceiling in the formation of an obscene picture or the fire your advisees set in the wastepaper basket before they inserted it into the air vents. Their silence on matters such as these and their cooperation in keeping the rooms well supplied and in good working order are worth a few kind words and small gifts from you.

CONCLUSION

As should be evident from the information contained in this chapter, the classroom teacher must not only be well versed in her subject matter but must be an expert in human relations and diplomacy as well. While conveying knowledge about subject matter should be the teacher's first concern, she must remember that her classroom and her attempts to educate her pupils do not exist in a vacuum. Her inability to relate satisfactorily to those around her will undoubtedly decrease her effectiveness in the classroom. Of a more practical and selfish nature is the fact that since the teacher spends the majority of her waking hours in school, it would be to her advantage to create pleasant working conditions and satisfying personal relationships for herself. With all the things the new teacher must learn, the novice would be wise to remain as unobtrusive and obscure as possible until time and experience show her who she can rely upon and how she can relate satisfactorily to all segments of the school community.

Chapter Eleven

Testing and Grading Procedures

Students and teachers both tend to feel that formal testing and grading are aspects of the standard educational process which they would like to see eliminated. The idealist feels that because of students' tendencies to view examinations as punitive measures rather than as learning experiences, she would prefer to find alternate means to written testing. The seasoned professional would agree with her but would readily admit that, unfortunately, workable alternatives have not yet been discovered which are practical for use in urban classroom situations. Practicality and tradition demand that standardized evaluation procedures must be administered. Prospective employers and schools of higher learning are concerned with the quality of the student's achievement and they expect to receive standardized reports in the form of numerical averages or letter grades and, in some cases, both.

Testing experts have estimated that more than one hundred and fifty million tests are administered annually in the normal functioning of educational programs. These tests represent an incalculable amount of time spent in planning and grading. The novice should feel justified in having numerous questions concerning what kind of tests are suitable for secondary school pupils, what functions each perform, how a teacher can be certain the tests are measuring what they are supposed to measure and how one constructs, administers and grades tests to insure reliability and validity.

KINDS OF TESTS

Oral Tests

The term test is a very general one. Any procedure a teacher uses to evaluate a pupil's learning experiences can be considered a test. When a teacher calls upon a student to answer a question orally in class she is, in a sense, administering a test. She is attempting to discover how much of what has just transpired in class the individual has assimilated and understood. However, even the beginner must realize that one question and one answer is an insufficient method for testing a pupil's over-all knowledge or for evaluating the learning experiences of the entire class. It only shows the amount of learning done by one student about one specific point of information. Such random questioning is useful in providing instant feedback on what the class seems to be learning about a subject area the teacher has just explained but that is its only value as a testing or evaluating tool. It is not very valid as a means for testing what the entire class knows or even how much the individual pupil understands and can use.

Another type of oral evaluation procedure requires every member of the class to relate some information to the group often in the form of a book review, speech or report. Students should always be warned in advance when they will be expected to perform this type of activity. It is unfair to force oral work on them without giving them time to prepare themselves intellectually and emotionally.

Oral evaluation has two major drawbacks. The first is that students are often so nervous when they are being evaluated in front of, and by, their peers that they do not perform well. For this reason, oral tests should never be the sole criteria upon which to judge a pupil's competency in a subject area. A second fault in the oral testing method lies in the fact that while one student is performing orally, thirty or forty students are crossing their eyes at him, making obscene hand gestures, eating their lunches or talking. To prevent this, the teacher should devise some method for keeping the rest of the class occupied and learning while their classmate is speaking. One method for doing this is to have the class take notes on the speeches and quiz them on them later. Another is to allow them to ask questions at the end of the speeches. In grading this type of test, the teacher would be wise to be as liberal as possible. Since most students are very nervous when they are called upon to talk to the class, the teacher should base her grades on the content of the student's report and not on the manner of presentation. Of course, if you are teaching a course designed to teach public speaking, the latter suggestion does not apply.

Essay Tests

A more formalized type of examination is the essay test. This type of test is useful because it permits the student and the teacher to exercise some freedom in the choice of material used. In an essay test, the teacher is not only able to evaluate a student's knowledge of subject matter, but how clearly he can express himself in writing. In an essay test, the student is forced to use the material he has learned and combine it with elements of his own personality, experience and point of view. This test is useful in helping the teacher to learn things about her students which might not be revealed in the course of normal classroom conversation. However, this type of examination should not be used unless the teacher has taught the class how to take an essay examination. One of the main limitations of the essay examination is that many secondary school pupils are not intellectually mature enough to take this type of test. They are unable to discipline themselves to answer only the question posed for them. They tend to throw everything they know into the answer that is even remotely related to the subject hoping that the reader will be able to detect the correct answer for herself. Some students wander so far from the original question in their answers that the teacher often feels forced to wonder what test the pupil was taking since his answers don't even remotely resemble any questions asked on the test she administered.

Another problem with the essay test is that the results are not often reliable. The chances are quite strong that several teachers discussing the same subject matter who read the same test paper will evaluate the essay answer differently. Furthermore, while it is relatively easy to detect which essay answers are above average and which are inferior, it is very difficult to tell if an essay answer is worth 82 points or 84 points. When you must figure out numerical averages at the end of each report period you will find yourself hard-pressed to know whether to average a B plus as an 87 or an 89. While this might seem very trivial now, when you find yourself in a teaching situation where competition for scholarships, awards and positions in the graduating class is extremely high, even decimal points become vital in determining who wins honors and scholarships, and you might be called upon to explain or defend your grades.

Because of the abundance of extraneous material often included in essay answers, the teacher would be wise to make a checklist of points she expects to be mentioned in every answer. Each answer should be compared with the checklist. Credit should be given for correct answers as well as points detracted for extraneous and irrelevant material. The teacher should make a concerted effort to discourage students from writing more than is necessary for selfish reasons as well as for the student's own benefit and training.

While an essay test is relatively easy to construct and a good question might come to you as you're brushing your teeth in the morning, driving to school or even discussing the course material with a friend, essay examinations take a very long time to grade. If a teacher has thirty to forty students in a class and each writes two or three pages, the teacher has close to a hundred pages of writing to read and comment upon. Often, it takes more than a single reading of a paper to evaluate its merit and a teacher should try to skim the entire set of class papers before grading any of them. Therefore, a teacher can spend most of her waking hours outside of the classroom reading and grading essay examinations. For practical, as well as educational reasons, the teacher would be wise to discourage the inclusion of any unnecessary material in essay test answers. She would also be wise to stagger the essay tests she administers. Most teachers teach five classes a day. If a teacher gave essay tests to all of her five classes in one week, she would be homebound grading exams for an entire week with only a few short breaks to warm up TV dinners and to have her eyes refracted. When the teacher gives an essay test to one class, she should try to give objective or oral examinations to her other classes. She can stagger the classes to which she gives the tests so that all have an opportunity to practice expressing themselves in a variety of testing situations.

Objective Tests

Objective examinations can take three major forms: the true-false, the completion and the multiple-choice examination. The type preferred by most professional testers is the multiple-choice form in which the student is required to select the correct answer to the question from several choices, usually four, offered by the teacher. This type of examination is preferred because it does not lend itself to guess-work as much as the true-false type does and it is not as ambiguous as the fill-in-the-blank, or completion type of question.

The multiple-choice test takes a very long time to construct. First, the teacher must be certain to select choices which take the same grammatical form. Changing grammatical forms might confuse the pupil or indicate which answer you had in mind when you made up the question. Next, she must be certain that the four choices are plausible. One choice should be unquestionably wrong. Two should be possible and only one should be definitely correct. The benefit of this type of test for the teacher lies in the fact that while it requires a lot of work to prepare, it is very easy to grade. A teacher need not even grade these papers herself. Since all the student writes on his answer sheet is the number or letter of his chosen answer, a teacher who has made up an answer key can grade long tests in a matter of a few minutes. She can have a friend, husband or relative who is not busy help her grade them quickly. It is not a good idea to have a student grade them for you as the ease of changing answers is too unfair a temptation to place on a student. It is wise also to have your students take these tests in ink rather than pencil. This is so that students will not be able to erase the incorrect answer and replace it with the correct one when you review the correct answers in class after the test papers have been graded and returned. If they make a mistake while taking the test, it is better for them to cross it out. When you see a crossed-out answer that a student claims you graded incorrectly, you will have to judge the student and your relationship with him to determine if he is telling the truth. However, you should always stress the importance of being certain about answers before making any selection. This should cut down on the number of crossed-out answers and make the necessity for your having to evaluate pupils' post test-taking honesty less likely.

Standardized Tests

The final type of examination which the teacher might be called upon to give is the standardized test. These tests are secured by the school districts to evaluate such things as the pupil's Intelligence Quotient (I.Q.), his reading ability, his aptitudes, and, in some areas, his scientific and mathematical ability. These tests are used to group students according to their ability levels and to reflect on a city-wide or school-wide basis how effective the educational system is. In some school systems these tests are graded by computers. In others, the individual teachers have to grade them with keys given to them by the testing company. Once the grades have been computed the teachers are required to record the grades on the pupil's permanent records which are stored in the school's administrative offices and which follow the students through their public school years.

Before administering a standardized test, be certain that you read the directions carefully and understand them. Then go over the sample problems and directions with the students to be certain that they understand what they are supposed to be doing. If the papers are to be graded by machines, be certain that you stress the importance of using the special pencils which are provided by the grading corporation or the papers will pass through the computers ungraded. While the test is being taken, it would be a good idea for you to circulate throughout the room to be certain that the students are following the instructions, filling out the question sheets properly and using the correct writing implements. It will save you a lot of time later and will prevent you from having to recopy your pupils' papers or grade them by hand.

TEST ADMINISTRATION

There are as many things to consider in administering a test as there are in constructing the test. First, it is important that the test be reasonable in length and difficulty. Before giving a test, a teacher should try to take the test herself. This should be done at least several hours, if not several days, after she has organized the test. If she cannot answer her own questions or if it takes her longer than half the amount of time allotted to her students to take the test, she should revise the test. Do not expect students to stay after class to finish an examination. This makes them late for their next class and makes it difficult for their next teacher, and for the other teacher who must use your room, to begin teaching on time.

Determine how you are going to give the test questions to the students in advance. Writing them on the board, especially if there are more than two or three questions, takes up a lot of class time. It also gives students in the back of the room the opportunity to stand up and look over their neighbors' shoulders at their papers while claiming that they were only trying to see the questions on the board. Reading the questions orally is not a better alternative. Students are very clever at organizing cheating signals. The best student in the class sneezes or nods once to the answer if the question is true and does nothing if it is false. In a multiple choice examination, students nod or smile when the correct choice is read. They can "compare" their answers with their neighbors' very easily because they are assured that they are all working on the same item at the same time. Another drawback of orally administering a test is the fact that it keeps the teacher occupied for the entire period. She is unable to see what is going on in the back of the room while her face is turned toward the question sheet.

The best way of administering test questions is to have them rex-o-graphed or xerographed before class begins. They can be given to the students as they enter the room if the questions are self-explanatory or you can wait until the class is seated and quiet before you distribute the papers and go over the directions. Be certain that you only count out one exam sheet for each pupil and that there are none left over. No extras should remain at the end of the row. Count out the papers carefully. Students who have extra question sheets will be very tempted to keep them and give them or sell them to friends in other classes or in lower grades.

If you are giving an objective test, you would be wise to have the students write their answers on separate sheets of paper. This makes it easier for you to grade the tests because you can read the answers down a straight column. It also enables you to use the same question sheets again. Be certain, however, before you attempt to use them again that you check them to see that the students have not checked the correct or incorrect answers on the sheets or written obscene messages on the reverse sides of the pages.

Do not make the mistake of giving the same test to different classes during the same day or even the same semester. The students will definitely meet in the halls and lunchrooms to brief their friends on what to expect.

If the rows of desks in your classroom are close together and are immovable, you would be wise to give neighboring rows different test questions, or different copies of the same test. If you are giving multiple choice questions or true and false items, change the numbers of the questions and make two forms of the test. This will prevent neighbors from copying, exchanging or checking answers with each other.

When you collect objective tests, try to stand in the middle of the room and supervise the collection procedure. Often, when objective tests are passed from one student to another, pupils in difficulty fill in the blanks on their own papers with suggestions from those of their peers.

Never leave a class alone when they are taking a test. This is a bad practice, aside from the obvious reason that it encourages cheating. A teacher should never leave a class alone for any reason. If trouble were to occur in the teacher's absence she would be held responsible and would face harsher repercussions than if she had been present. It is also necessary for the teacher to remain in the room to answer any questions the students might have while they are taking the examination.

While the teacher should be able to sit down to grade some papers or read a magazine while her class is taking a test, she should not totally ignore the group. She should walk around the room periodically to be certain that the students are not answering the questions by referring to notes they have hidden on their legs and written on their palms or failing to follow test directions. If she does read while the class is working, she would be wise to sit in the back of the room instead of at the front. This way, the students are never certain if they are being watched and they tend to be more honest in their test-taking techniques.

Grading

GRADING PAPERS

Homework and test papers should be graded promptly and returned to the students as soon as possible. Occasionally it will be impractical to return papers as soon as you have graded them because absentees have not yet been tested. While you should not give absentees the same tests you gave to the class, since they covered the same material, their tests will, of necessity, be similar. Therefore, you should not re-turn or review test papers until the entire class has taken the test. If it is an important test and the students are under-standably anxious to know about their grades you might post the grades on a bulletin board in the classroom. To avoid embarrassing the poorer students, the teacher should assign a number to each student. Tell each student his number privately by whispering it to him while the class is working silently or by writing the names and numbers on slips of paper and giving one to each pupil. Then, after each exam has been graded, you can post the grades beside each number. Pupils deserve the consideration of anonymity. There is nothing they resent more than public humiliation. For this reason the teacher should also refrain from reading compo-sitions and test answers to the class in a mocking tone or from identifying the writers of works read aloud without permis-sion.

In grading papers, teachers should attempt to be as fair and impartial as possible. One way to do this is to read all the test papers at least once before grading any of them. This will give the teacher an idea of how fair her test was, how many were able to excel, how many could not finish all the problems and how many misunderstood the questions. This practice will prevent the teacher from realizing half way through grading a set of papers that the test was too hard or too long or that her standards were too high.

Never try to grade an entire set of papers at one time. If you do, you will discover that you are either too liberal or too critical of those papers which you grade when you are tired. Try to divide your grading chores into two or three sessions, depending upon the number and length of the papers you have to grade. Before beginning to grade the second and third groups of papers, go back and review the first briefly to be certain that your grading standards remain consistent.

In composition papers, a teacher should not attempt to point out every error. Some papers come back so filled with red marks that the students cannot read their original remarks. In addition, it is good practice to try to find something to commend in every paper. In some papers this will be especially difficult and you will find yourself grasping for ideas with comments such as "That's a nice color of ink you used," or "you clipped your papers together exceptionally well." Finding something to commend in all of your pupils' work is very difficult but it is good educational practice because it encourages students who might otherwise be totally discouraged by a paper full of negative comments to continue to try to improve.

When it is feasible, a teacher should attempt to give two grades for each paper, one grade representing the content of the paper and the other representing the form. Very often a pupil will write a composition which is grammatically and structurally correct but extremely dull and unimaginative. A pupil will use all the correct theories or equations in solving mathematics problems or testing chemical formulas and come up with the wrong answers because he cannot add columns of numbers or because he makes a minor mistake at the beginning of his work. Giving two grades focuses the pupil's attention dramatically on the specific area of his failures.

When a teacher constructs a test, she should bear in mind that it will have to be graded. Inane as this sounds, many new teachers find themselves with a class set of true and false tests containing 77 questions and no plan for computing the over-all paper grade. Since there is no way to give every question equal weight, the educator is in a quandary when she must determine how many correct answers equal an A, a B and so on down the line.

Since a testing situation should also serve as a learning experience, the teacher should be cautious about when and under what circumstances she returns papers. Papers should not be returned while students are noisy and inattentive or when only a few minutes remain in a class period. They should be returned when there is sufficient time to go over the right answers to the questions and explain how those correct answers should have been computed. If papers are returned at the end of the period when only a few minutes of class remain, students will forget to bring them back to class for a later discussion and will have accepted their classmates' incorrect explanations of why their answer was wrong and their friend's was right and, thus, will have no reason to listen to your explanations later. In such situations, a valuable learning opportunity is lost.

When graded papers are returned to a class, the teacher should take special care not to embarrass a student or allow his privacy to be invaded. Other students should not know what grades their classmates received. When returning papers, do not give them to students to pass to each other with the grades showing. Either give each paper to the pupil individually or pass it to the student with the paper folded over in such a way that the passers cannot see the grade. Never read an answer aloud to the class for the purpose of commending or degrading it with the pupil's name visible. Even if a paper is extremely good or inspiring, do not reveal the writer's name without obtaining his permission first.

Be careful about giving extra credit work. Students who are doing poorly in a course should not be given extra credit assignments. If a pupil cannot do the assigned required work in an acceptable manner he should have no time or ability to do any extra work. All of his efforts should be expended in trying to meet the requirements of the course, not trying to circumvent them with other assignments. Furthermore, it is difficult to grade extra credit work. How does a teacher reflect the grade of a pupil who does all of the extra credit assignments carefully and accurately while failing in all of his required work? Often, allowing a poor student to do extra assignments is encouraging him falsely and taking valuable time away from his regular classwork assignments. Extra assignments should be devised for students who deviate from the class norm in ability or interest but these should take the form of assignments which are different from what the class is doing rather than in addition to what the class is doing. The logic behind this is that if the student is superior in ability to the rest of the class, he should not be bored by doing what the more average students are doing. If his learning skills are inferior to his peers, he should not be frustrated by being forced to do the work chosen for his classmates' needs.

Do not hesitate to admit that you made a mistake if your test questions prove too difficult or unfair for your students. When you discover that no one had the opportunity to finish all of the questions or the majority of the class got the fifth question wrong, you should reexamine your test. If the reevaluation leads you to believe that you were wrong, do not make your students suffer for your error. Give each student enough credit to compensate for your error. However, if you are certain that the failure rightfully belongs with your students because they weren't paying attention or following your directions, do not retract your grades under pressure from them to do so.

While it is a good idea to see how your grades are distributed, it is not wise to try to alter your grades to fit into the mythological U-shaped curve. The curve theory is based upon the idea that you should have the same number of A's as you have failures, the same number of B's as D's and the majority of the grades should fall in the C category. The second largest grouping should be the B-D segments with the fewest grades falling in the A-F section. The chances of this type of grade distribution occurring automatically are very slim. Trying to force this pattern is unwise. U-shaped curves do not normally occur in groupings as small as the thirty or forty pupils you have in your classes. Trying to impose one would be unfair to your students and not a true reflection of their abilities. The only instances in which grades should be distributed into some kind of pattern are those in which you find that almost everyone has failed a test or everyone has gotten an A indicating that your questions were much too easy or much too difficult. Obviously, students will react more favorably to changes raising their grades than to those lowering their scores.

Before you grade your first set of papers, it would be a good idea for you to check with your department chairman to see if the school maintains any definite policies on grading. Some schools insist that slow students not be given grades higher than D on their report cards unless the teacher is prepared to recommend them for average sections. The philosophy behind this type of mandate is that if a student is capable of earning a grade of C or better, he has been misplaced in a slow section and should be moved to his proper grouping. Many schools insist also that students in advanced or rapid groups should only be given grades of B or higher. The philosophy here is like that of the slow groups. If a student is not capable of earning a grade above the average C, then he does not belong in a rapid section and should be transferred back to an average group. Many schools insist that pupils who have been placed into special sections doing college level work should be given A's because they are superior to their classmates who are following the regular high school curriculum even if they are not superior to their exceptional peers. You must know about these policies in advance, although they should never be made public to the pupils. If you give slow pupils A's in the quizzes and D's on their report cards, you will have a very difficult time justifying your actions. If your school does maintain such mandatory grading policies, you would be wise to grade your slow students' papers on a pass-fail basis. With your rapid classes, the problem is not quite as acute. Students are not very likely to complain if their test and composition grades reflect their actual standing in their class and their higher report card grades reflect their standing in the school population.

RECORD KEEPING

One of the more tedious jobs a classroom teacher must perform is the maintenance of clear, accurate records. She has to keep the students' permanent cumulative records up to date and she must maintain an accurate, detailed set of personal records reflecting the achievement of the pupils in each of her individual classes. This latter part of her clerical duties is not very easy to accomplish even if she is normally a methodical, meticulous person. It is so difficult to do because the teacher must record classwork, quizzes, major examinations and absences almost daily. Doing this without confusing the major and minor grades is not a simple task. School districts provide their teachers with grade books for their individual use but most of these books are only divided into many little squares. The teacher must devise a clear system for using these squares to her best advantage. One way to record all the pupils' grades and differentiate between the major and minor ones is to use different pages in the book for recording tests, quizzes, classwork and oral work. Another way is to record the different types of grades in different color ink. Attendance can be kept in pencil on a separate sheet or even in a different book. Some people use letter grades (A-F) for oral work, numerical grades for major tests, numerical grades on a 1-10 scale for quizzes and pluses (+) and minuses (−) for classwork drills. Whichever system you use, be certain that you label all of your grades at the top or bottom of the columns in your record book so that you can identify them later. Also record the date on which the work was administered so you can help your absentees make up what they missed when they return to class.

Companies who publish materials specifically for teachers and educational supply houses located in major cities handle mark books with spaces for recording all of the facets of a pupil's progress. Books of this type are worth the investment because they greatly simplify the teacher's job.

After grading a set of papers, enter the grades in your mark book in pencil. This is done in case you've made an error in grading which a student might point out to you when you are reviewing the papers with the class or in the event that you decide to give credit for a problem the class convinces you was marked too strictly or unfairly. After all of the papers have been returned and discussed, go over your pencil grades in ink.

Any teacher who has been through the experience of losing a grade book or having it stolen from her car or desk will tell you that there is nothing more frightening or upsetting, especially if it occurs right before report card grades are due to be submitted. There is really nothing a teacher can do to remedy this situation once it has occurred. Her students will never be able to return all of their graded papers to her. Many will have been lost or discarded. Trying to reconstruct several weeks or months worth of grades for over a hundred pupils is a total impossibility. To prevent yourself from ever being caught in this highly undesirable situation, always maintain two copies of your students' grades. One copy of your mark book should be kept safely at home—never brought to school, the hairdresser's or your doctor's office with you. If you grade papers in school during your free period, bring the grade book you use at school home with you and copy the grades into the book stored at home. While this takes a little extra time, anyone who has lost her only copy of her grade book, or has had it stolen from her desk or car will tell you that it is worth every minute you have spent making the additional copy to have this insurance.

Report card grades are given out three or four times a year. Find out when the closing dates for entering these grades are as soon as you are settled into the routine of your new position. Many urban high schools have computerized their report card grade distribution system. Each teacher is given an IBM sheet for her pupils on which she enters their report card grades. All of the sheets are fed through a computer and, almost miraculously, the report cards are returned to the teachers with all the different subject matter grades recorded in their proper places. Since many schools in the system must use the same computer, the grades often have to be submitted as far in advance as a month before the report card grades are ready to be given to the pupils. This presents quite a problem since any work done in the weeks after the grades are entered is not reflected in the grade the pupil takes home to his parents. This becomes confusing for both parents and students. It presents many difficulties for the teacher also, particularly at the end of the semester. The students know that the grades have been submitted and even though you continue to admonish them that they can be changed by hand up to the last minute, they rarely believe that you will do so. Try to save your most stimulating lessons for this time when students are anxious to get out of school and begin their vacations and are confidently resting on the knowledge that their grades have already been submitted.

Parents are justified in coming to see teachers to discuss their children's progress. Teachers should be prepared to reveal the basis upon which they decided which grades to assign to each pupil. Parents deserve explanations of the reasons behind their children's failures or lack of improvement. When the professional discusses a student's achievement with a parent he should be certain to be as specific as possible, to make positive suggestions as well as negative comments and to avoid discussing the work of any other pupil.

Report card grades can be assigned by taking into consideration one of two criteria: overall averages of work done by the pupils during the entire marking period or on the basis of improvement. If a student is inconsistent in his work, doing well one week, poorly the next, and excelling the third, the best thing to do would be to take an average of all of his grades. A student who, on the other hand, fails most of his assignments during the early weeks, then suddenly understands what the teacher has been talking about and begins achieving high grades should not be penalized for what he did not understand before but is capable of using efficiently at the end of the year. When there is any question about a grade, however, the teacher is safest when she can point to numerical averages to substantiate the grade she has assigned. She must not allow personal prejudices in favor of, or against, a pupil to influence her in computing these grades. The teacher wields a tremendous power over a pupil's life because the report card grade she assigns will make a difference in the student's class standing and affect his ability to win a scholarship, a job or qualify to continue his education. For this reason the teacher should be extremely careful not to allow her personal feelings to interfere with her objectivity.

Constructing, administering, grading and recording pupils' work are among the educator's more tedious jobs. It would be to the teacher's advantage to make these chores as pleasant for herself as possible by conceiving tests which are interesting to read as well as easy to grade. Her records should be accurate, clearly interpreted and kept up to date. She must constantly remember that at any moment a counselor, parent or administrator might ask to see her records of her pupils' achievements. Such people are justified in their requests and, while you should never discuss another student's work with his peers, you should be prepared to confer about a pupil's progress with those people who are entitled to know about it whenever you are asked to do so.

The most important thing a teacher must consider when she prepares her tests and assigns grades to those tests and to the semester's work is that her evaluations will affect her students' entire lives. How well a student does in a particular course will often help to determine what career he selects for himself, if he is admitted to the college of his choice, and if he gets the job he applied for. Furthermore, his grades influence his opinion of himself as a human being and alter his estimation of his achievement potential. Therefore, a teacher should examine both her tests and her grades to be certain that her personal prejudices, problems and interests are not affecting her judgment of a student's capabilities and potentials or preventing him from gaining what is rightfully his. This cannot be emphasized too strongly. In a way, when a teacher evaluates a pupil, she is playing the role of God in judging the value of another human being. Since she does not possess the deep insight attributed to God, she must make a concerted effort to have as broad a basis and as opened and unprejudiced a point of view as she possibly can when she passes judgment upon another human being's achievements.

Commonly Used Testing Terms With Which the Educator Should Be Familiar:

achievement test—an examination which evaluates the extent to which a student has learned a skill or information.

age norms—scores which reflect the typical or average ability for students of different age groups. These are used in comparing the results of standardized test scores in subjects such as reading and mathematics.

aptitude—a combination of skills and interests which indicate a student's ability in a particular field.

average—the total of a set of test scores divided by the number of tests taken.

completion test—a set of questions which requires the student to supply a word or phrase which has been omitted from the statements put forth by the tester.

diagnostic test—an examination designed to discover a student's strength and weaknesses. These are used by teachers to decide what a student has to learn and what he already knows.

essay test—an examination which permits a student to have some freedom in the kind and amount of information he uses to answer a teacher's question. The pupil expresses his thoughts in sentences and paragraphs and often reveals his personality and point of view through the type of material he selects and the manner in which he presents it.

grade norm—the scores which reflect the average grade obtained by pupils of a specific grade level.

intelligence quotient (IQ)—literally, the ratio of a student's mental age to his chronological age. It is basically a scale for reflecting a person's ability to learn which takes into account the results of intelligence tests and the age of the student.

item or question analysis—the procedure of evaluating individual test questions to determine their difficulty and fairness. This is often done by making charts to see how many pupils answer each question correctly.

matching test—an examination in which the students are required to associate information on one list with items on a second list.

median—the middle score in the results of a set of tests. Half of the tested group receives grades which are higher than this point and half will be lower.

mental age (MA)—the age for which a given score on an intelligence test is normal.

mode—the grade which is received by more members of a tested group than any other.

norms—the numbers which reflect the test results of specific groups such as students of the same age or grade. They reveal the average performance of the members of these groups.

objective test—an examination in which there is only one right answer which is usually expressed as a few words, a number, a letter, or a choice of true or false.

readiness test—an examination which evaluates a student's maturity and previous learning experiences to determine if he is capable of attempting a new learning activity.

reliability—the extent to which an examination is consistent in measuring whatever it was designed to evaluate.

true-false test—an examination in which the student must determine whether a statement is correct or incorrect.

validity—the extent to which a test measures what it was intended to measure.

Chapter Twelve

Supportive Services Available to the Teacher

The teacher in secondary education is expected to fulfill many roles in addition to that of educator during her working hours. School district recruiters often emphasize the fact that they expect their employees to do more than teach English, mathematics, physical education or art. They make it very clear to those whom they interview that they require their teachers to constantly remember that they were hired to educate young people not to merely teach subject matter. Novices are directed to concentrate on teaching children not on teaching books, drills, and lesson plans. The latter are only tools for achieving the broad goal of educating the total human being so that he can find a place for himself as a satisfied, complete, contributing member of society. In essence, what this means is that the teacher at the secondary school level must wear many different "hats." She functions in the roles of friend, advisor, educator, temporary parent, disciplinarian, adversary, psychologist, psychiatrist and sometimes physician. This is a gargantuan task for any human being to attempt to handle. Fortunately, the educator is not alone in her quest to meet all of the needs of all of her students. School districts provide a wide variety of supportive services to help alleviate some of the pressures upon the classroom teacher to help her to satisfy the broad needs of each of the individuals in her classes. Community and national groups offer forms of assistance also.

In addition to those services and facilities which are available to the students, many districts provide professional services which enable the teacher to improve herself as an educator and to expand her awareness of the world in which she functions so that she can achieve her full potential as a human being. The professional services are often supplemented by medical and financial assistance programs subsidized or totally supported by the school district.

The numbers, types, structures, and names assigned to the various supportive services will, of necessity, vary from location to location. Most major educational systems will offer all of the services discussed in this chapter. The smaller ones usually join together in cooperating to share the facilities and the personnel with the many schools in their area. The novice has so much to learn about the students she must teach, the material she must cover and the school routines to which she must adjust that she cannot hope to learn all about the supportive services her school district offers as soon as she begins her assignment. The administration will not expect this of her and she should not demand it of herself. In the beginning of your teaching experiences it is sufficient for you to know what services should be available and what services are normally offered by school systems to their students and teachers. Then, as the need for the facilities arises, you can inquire about the existence of the particular assistance you or your pupils require and the manner used for obtaining this help from your colleagues, department head or principal.

GUIDANCE

Teen-agers, more so than any other students, seem to have an abundance of emotional problems. Most of these problems are justified. Adolescence is a very difficult period. Children are expected to become emotionally, physically and intellectually mature all at once. Often, they do not reach maturity in all three levels at one time which further adds to their difficulties. The six-foot-tall boy with the mustache he proudly displays to his peers still likes to throw confetti out of the window. The girl who is physically underdeveloped does well in her major subjects but fails physical education because she refuses to change into her gym clothes in front of her classmates. The pupils who are socially advanced cannot wait to tell their friends about their sexual exploits and adventures into the worlds of alcohol consumption and drug use. Yet, their reading comprehension is three steps below their grade levels. And the boy who receives high grades on all his tests refuses to answer any questions orally in class because his classmates giggle when his voice changes pitch suddenly.

The pressures of growing up physically, socially and emotionally are compounded by the fact that during their years in secondary schools, students must make decisions which will affect the shape of their futures. Early in the secondary grades they must select a curriculum which will determine whether they enter a trade, business field, college program or homemaking environment when they complete their schooling. This is a momentous decision for a student to have to make, particularly when you consider the fact that your pupils are relatively inexperienced and have no sound basis on which to make a choice about what direction their lives are going to take or should take.

In addition to the problems just discussed which are encountered by most of the young people you teach, there are those members of your classes who have additional burdens to carry. Some suffer from physical handicaps and chronic illnesses which necessitate long or frequent absences. Others have financial problems which cause them to dress shabbily and take one or two after-school jobs. And still others have family problems which make it difficult for them to concentrate on their studies or attend classes on a regular basis.

To be effective, it is extremely important that the classroom teacher be aware of the difficulties faced by students. Most adults, when looking back on their junior and senior high school days, seem only to remember the proms and football games. Many fail to remember the tension and confusion of being treated like a child while having to carry some of the responsibilities of an adult. For a large percentage of the student body, the pressures students face are too great for them to handle alone. Some students receive all the assistance they need from their families. These are the fortunate ones. The others turn to the professional for help, to their friends or attempt to carry their burdens alone, often failing in their school work as a result.

The classroom teacher cannot be expected to have the insight or the time required to handle all of these individual problems. What she should be able to do, however, is to take the time to really listen to her students, not only to what they say but to what they don't say as well. Some students withdraw and do not discuss their problems with their teachers but need as much help as their more vocal peers. After listening to her pupils, the educator should indicate that she is interested in the problem, understands the situation and is willing to refer the pupil to the person most qualified to give him the assistance he requires.

All modern schools provide guidance personnel to help teachers assist their students with their individual problems. Some students will take the initiative of asking their counselors for help with course selection, adjustment problems, financial difficulties and emotional problems. These professionals are infinitely more qualified to cope with these problems on an individual basis. They have information on community and social agencies as well as on trade schools and universities readily accessible to them. They have facilities for conferring privately with pupils and their parents and for testing vocational and learning skills which are not available to individual teachers or which are superior to those provided for teachers. Therefore, problems and potential problems should be referred to the school guidance personnel as soon as the educator detects them.

Unfortunately, because of the size of most urban high schools, the number of guidance counselors provided by the school districts is far below the number required to meet the needs of the entire student body. In some schools the ratio of guidance personnel to students is as high as one counselor to every eight or nine hundred pupils. Because of this fact, the teacher should do all that she can to handle those minor problems she can cope with effectively without involving the guidance staff. She would be wise, after the hectic opening weeks of school have passed, to meet with one of the guidance staff to learn about the functions the counselors in her school are capable of performing and about the community social organizations which are available to help her pupils. This will enable her to sort out those problems which the counselors can handle and to direct students to the proper agencies to help them with their individual problems.

As a basis for her inquiries, the novice should direct her investigations into several distinct types of services. She should be concerned with those agencies which provide facilities for students who are mentally or physically handicapped. These include local branches of nationwide organizations such as the National Cystic Fibrosis Foundation, American Diabetes Association, and Muscular Dystrophy Association as well as clinics which offer free medical care and dispense objects such as eyeglasses and crutches at no cost or for a minimal rate. She should learn of those agencies which cope with emotional problems. These involve not only problems of the students themselves but of their families. Alcoholics Anonymous, the Veterans Administration, the Shriners, and the Jewish Family Service are examples of this type of agency which can be suggested to parents or students who are in need of the services they provide. Many local church and religious groups also offer assistance with personal problems. However, only the guidance personnel in the individual schools can tell you what these groups are in your location and what they can and will do for your students. Some will even help with financial problems by providing clothing, food and scholarships for destitute families in their area if these difficulties are called to their attention by the school.

From what has been said thus far on the subject of guidance, it would appear that the classroom teacher is a social worker as well as an educator. This impression is not very far from the truth. The more a teacher can do to help her students with their individual difficulties, the easier it is for her to function as a teacher of a subject matter area. The most obvious reason for this is that her students will be able to concentrate better if their minds are relieved of some of the pressures on them and for the less obvious reason that the relationship between students and teacher will be strengthened by the educator's personal interest in her pupils' lives. However, it cannot be stressed too strongly that the teacher should not attempt to be all things to all people. Her principal responsibility is that of teaching a specific subject to her pupils as effectively as possible in the amount of time which is allotted to her to do so. Frequent digressions to handle individual cases will prevent her from doing this. The teacher, then, must be prepared to delegate many of her guidance chores to those who are more qualified to handle them. She must be aware of her own limitations in this area. While she should make every effort to be as informed as she can about the agencies available to her classes, she should not let her concern for her pupils' personal problems interfere with her effectiveness as a teacher, and she should not be reluctant to admit that she does not know how to help a pupil and to refer him to his assigned guidance counselor for assistance. Whenever she does this, however, she should follow up the results of their meetings to be certain the pupil got the help he needed, to learn what was done for him and to discover what she might do herself in a similar situation, should it arise again.

MEDICAL

Almost all schools have permanent full-time nurses in the building during school hours. Many larger schools also have doctors present. However, these physicians usually serve several schools, spending a few hours in each one every week. These doctors examine the members of the school teams, such as football, basketball and swimming, every semester. They give thorough physical examinations to the rest of the student body at prescribed intervals such as every two or three years. These examinations enable the school district to locate those students with communicable diseases such as tuberculosis and ringworm, with physical abnormalities such as overweight, poor posture, heart murmurs, weak eyesight and with nervous disorders such as tics and tremors. These individuals are then referred to their private physicians for treatment or to clinics which are equipped to handle their cases. A check is later made to be certain that students received the treatment they needed and that those who are contagious are not permitted to return to school until they can no longer infect others. The school physicians or nurses will take care of reporting all communicable diseases to the proper authorities so the teacher does not have to be concerned about this.

Most of the illnesses or injuries which occur in school can be handled by the nurse. She is the one who puts bandages on scraped knees, straps sprained ankles and dispenses aspirins by the hundreds. She is also qualified to administer first aid in the event of an emergency. If a student is seriously injured in your presence, if he is unconscious or bleeding, do not attempt to move him. Send a responsible student to the nurse or to the main office if your school does not have a nurse constantly in attendance. Be certain that he is instructed to tell the nurse or the secretary exactly what has happened and what condition the patient appears to be in. This will tell her what equipment she must bring and whether she should send for an ambulance or the local doctor who has made himself readily available to the school for emergencies. Merely sending a student to bring the nurse without sending specific instructions to give to her only wastes valuable time because she might come without important equipment and have to go back to her office before she can give any assistance.

It would be to the teacher's advantage to learn something about emergency first aid also. You can never tell when a student might have a convulsion or fainting spell, or be stabbed, shot or knocked unconscious by a classmate in your room. Knowing how to stop bleeding or how to protect an epileptic from injuring himself until the nurse arrives could prevent serious injuries or fatalities from occurring.

In schools where the surrounding economic conditions are very poor, the services of the school nurse might be invoked to discuss the matter of personal hygiene and cleanliness. Difficult as it may be for the novice to believe, many students in poor rural and urban areas know very little about nutrition and maintaining healthy personal habits. One way to handle such discussions, should the teacher feel they are necessary, is to ask the nurse to speak to the female members of the class while the teacher meets with the boys in the library to work on a research project. The physician or a male teacher, possibly a physical education or hygiene teacher or a sports sponsor, might meet with the boys at a later date while the teacher works in the library with the female students.

Local hospitals can be depended upon to provide clinics and free medical care for those who cannot afford to pay for it. The school nurse can tell you when the clinics are open and how your students can make appointments. She can also tell you about special services the hospitals provide such as birth control clinics, courses in first aid and baby care and training courses for nurses' aides and orderlies.

In most large urban school districts, remedial physical education programs are provided for those with handicaps or disabilities. Often these programs are conducted by physical education teachers during the student's regularly-scheduled gym classes. In some situations, therapists visit the schools on a rotating basis one or two days a week. If this is the case in the school in which you are employed, you should be prepared to have students excused from your classes occasionally to attend their therapy sessions. While it is not very desirable to have a student miss your class it is extremely important that he be given every opportunity to overcome his handicaps.

Student service organizations and honor societies volunteer their services to help handicapped students. Pupils earn points toward awards by reading to blind students, helping them to classes and transporting books and supplies for handicapped pupils. Even if such services are not part of a student service club's regular schedule of activities, it is almost certain that the advisors of these groups will make arrangements to find students who would be willing to help your disabled student get to and from his classes and complete his assignments.

Occasionally a student will be stricken with an illness which will require him to stay out of school for a prolonged period of time. If he is going to be out for a week or two the teacher should try, depending upon the severity of the student's condition, to send assignments home with a reliable pupil or to phone them to the pupil or his parents. However, if a student's illness will keep him away from the classroom for several months or longer, your department head or principal should be consulted about the possibility of obtaining a "home-bound teacher" for the pupil. Larger school districts hire professional personnel who visit the homes of students who will be bedridden with noncontagious ailments which prevent them from attending classes for prolonged periods of time. Other systems arrange for the installation of communication systems which enable pupils to listen in to classroom lessons and, with some more advanced systems, even participate in discussions from his home. School department heads and principals should be consulted about the availability and procedures for obtaining the use of these facilities.

EDUCATIONAL

While the responsibility for educating the student body rests primarily with the classroom teacher, there are supportive personnel in the school system who will help her cope with individual learning problems. All teachers should arrange to have conference periods before or after school during which time she can meet with her pupils to give them personal help with work they do not understand or have missed as a result of illness. However, many students will need more help than you can give them in several after-school meetings. These pupils should have the services of a tutor in the subject area in which they are deficient. More affluent parents obtain tutors for their children frequently on their own initiative or at the suggestion of teachers. Pupils who cannot afford this luxury should be directed to contact the student tutoring groups which are often sponsored by school honor societies. If your school does not have such a group, it would be a good idea for you to suggest the formation of one or organize one on a school-wide or class-wide basis.

Parents can be very helpful in tutoring students also. Parent-Teacher Associations often have parent-tutoring groups established to assist teachers by instructing pupils before and after school and during their lunch periods. If the PTA in your school does not have such a program you might request volunteers by attending a meeting personally or by requesting your faculty representative to do so for you.

Parent-Teacher groups can also be very helpful educationally by providing money for facilities and experiments not funded by the regular school budget. These groups are constantly looking for worthwhile projects to work for and support financially. They will be willing to listen to your requests for their assistance in obtaining facilities for the betterment of the school's educational devices. Of course, their reactions are more likely to be favorable if your plan involves more than just your own classes. Teaching machines, tape recorders, sets of textbooks, and record players are examples of materials which can be shared by many teachers to enhance the learning experiences of the entire student body.

Teachers' colleges and universities often sponsor tutoring programs through their service clubs or as part of their

188

practice teaching curriculum. The schools in your area should be contacted about such plans if they are not already in use in your school.

Community groups should be considered when the teacher is searching for long-term added assistance for her classes. Church groups, the Black Panthers, the Young Lords and other community awareness groups are examples of the type of organizations which often plan tutoring programs for their community's young people who need such help.

Urban school districts employ professionals to work with students who have severe learning disabilities in one particular area. They also maintain special schools for students who are deaf, or blind, and who speak languages other than English as their native tongues or who exhibit severe emotional or behavioral abnormalities. Remedial speech and reading teachers are provided for pupils who have deficiencies in these areas. Rural areas supply personnel of this type too but rather than remaining in the school daily, they are shared by the many schools in the district and they visit them on a rotating basis. The subject area teacher should view her qualifications for coping with these particular difficulties realistically and realize her own limitations in handling these problems. Since, in most cases, she is not qualified to handle speech therapy or to deal with emotionally disturbed students, she should not attempt to accomplish these tasks. Her major responsibility to her pupils in these areas is to detect those students who are in need of the services of a specialist and to refer them to the proper person. She should check to be certain that the pupils and the specialists are following up on her recommendations and that the help she requested is being given. She should also try to watch the student's progress to see if the added work is accelerating his learning. It would be wise to confer with the specialist to see if there is something the teacher can do in the context of her lessons to help the student with his problem or to reinforce the additional learning experiences. If a learning disability appears to be prevalent in most of the students in any particular class, the classroom teacher might ask the specialist to visit her classroom occasionally to work with the class as a whole or to suggest some technique the educator can use to help all of her students.

Students who are in trade curriculums are frequently discipline and behavior problems in the academic courses they must take to fulfill state requirements for obtaining their diplomas. Courses which are most frequently mandated by state law include English, general mathematics and science courses, history or civics and physical education. Gym is rarely a problem but the same cannot be said for history, English and the general science and mathematics courses. Fortunately, students in trade curriculums are grouped together. This makes it easier for the teachers of the subjects mentioned above to focus their attention on meeting their students' needs and interests. Work-study programs are often set up for these pupils. They are organized so that students either attend classes for a portion of each school day and work at a paying job for the rest of the day or they attend classes all day one week and work a full day the next week. This type of program is a great source of motivation for the pupils and the teacher should make a concerted effort to relate her subject to the work being done by the pupils on their jobs.

Teachers should be alert for students in their classes who seem distracted or disinterested in their studies. These pupils are likely candidates for work-study programs. Often, members of trade unions or businesses which hire pupils on a part-time basis with a view toward permanent full-time employment upon graduation will send speakers to your classrooms who will help the students see the relevancy of your subject matter to their lives and will help to put their future plans into realistic perspectives. They will also tell the teacher what she can do, within the confines of her subject matter, to help prepare her pupils for their future vocations.

190

SERVICES FOR THE TEACHER'S INDIVIDUAL NEEDS

A considerable amount of attention has been directed thus far in this text to the great responsibilities the teacher has in meeting the needs of her pupils in as many areas of their development as she can educationally and professionally. However, as in most educational texts, the teacher herself has emerged as the "forgotten man or woman." Actually, this is not true. Most new teachers find themselves developing severe cases of paranoia somewhere around the third week of the semester which get progressively more severe until they imagine that their students are stabbing each other and sniffing glue just to spite them. These educators frequently begin talking to themselves shortly before Thanksgiving and are convinced that they will never make it to the mecca of their paid Christmas vacations. Fortunately for the students, the school districts and the teachers themselves, most educators not only last until Christmas but return to school in January with renewed strength and fresh perspectives which help them to do more than "ride with the punches." They find new insight and strength which gives them the courage to last until summer vacation and even to sign contracts to return next year.

The fact that most teachers manage to weather the first years of teaching can be attributed to more than the teacher's self-sacrificing dedication to her profession or her tendencies toward masochism. Part of the credit belongs to those services which aid the teacher in satisfying her own social, educational, financial and emotional needs.

School districts offer many services to provide for the teacher's well-being aside from her basic salary. They automatically deduct money from her paycheck which is applied toward health and welfare plans and, in some states, toward retirement programs. The deductions are usually subsidized by the school district or the state and the teacher receives medical coverage for herself and her family at rates far lower than she could independently. Money taken for retirement programs is also subsidized so that when the teacher retires or

191

resigns from the system she receives her money back with interest. Large systems offer life insurance policies at reduced rates, the premiums of which are also deducted from the paychecks. Many school districts will subtract payments for union dues and United States savings bonds automatically at the teacher's request. Because of the possibility of so many varied deductions, the new teacher would be wise to check with a secretary connected with the payroll department to find out exactly how much her take-home pay will actually be. This will prevent her from counting on having twenty or thirty dollars more to spend than she will actually receive.

Medical facilities are provided for the teacher's use in addition to the health and welfare plans just discussed. New teachers are given complete physical examinations by school district medical personnel before they are permitted to assume their positions. Periodic check-ups, chest X-rays and inoculations against epidemics are offered to teachers without cost. The same emergency medical aid that is available to students in the individual schools is available to the teachers.

School systems make provisions for teacher's illnesses which necessitate their absence from school through the use of "Sick Days." These are days given to the teacher to stay home from school in the event of illness without loss of pay. The number of "Sick Days" allotted varies from district to district so the teacher would be wise to find out how many days she is given and whether these days accumulate from year to year if they are not used. Often, when a teacher leaves the system she receives some financial compensation for the "Sick Days" she has not used. Ten days a year is the average number of days granted for teacher illnesses. Some more progressive school districts supplement teachers' "Sick Days" with "Personal Leave Days." These are days which are granted to the teachers to conduct personal business which cannot be handled at any other times. This includes things such as attending funerals, weddings and graduations, or participating in conferences and community activities. Two or three days a year is the usual number granted for these purposes and the teacher is also often compensated for the days not used when she leaves the system. However, these days do not usually accumulate if they are unused from term to term as the "Sick Days" traditionally do.

To stimulate their teachers intellectually, larger school districts offer in-service courses at no charge. These courses are conducted by school-district teachers or qualified outside experts hired by the district. They are held after school in centrally-located areas. The teacher can take courses in her own subject area or in any field she is interested in. Frequently, these courses give a teacher credit toward promotions and pay raises.

Many school districts will subsidize or lend the teacher the money needed to continue her education at local universities. In some cases, the amount a teacher must pay on a loan is reduced in relation to the number of years she continues to teach in the system.

After teaching for a given number of years, usually between five and ten, teachers can apply for leaves of absence for six months to a year during which time they can continue their educations on a full-time basis, write or travel. When such a leave is granted, the school district will continue to pay the educator a portion of her salary for living expenses and will hold her teaching position open for her until she returns.

Before accepting any permanent position, a teacher would be wise to inquire about the number, kind and quality of services and benefits offered to teachers by her prospective employers. The existence of these additional programs should be as important a consideration as the basic salary she is offered and the teaching conditions under which she must work.

Very large schools and schools located in the inner cities often have to cope with the problem of protecting the physical safety of their teachers and student body. To do this, some school districts hire retired or off-duty policemen, prison matrons, and ex-judo instructors to patrol the halls, lunchrooms, stairways, grounds around the building and nearby bus stops to eject or control intruders, gang members, and hostile students who present a potential threat to personal safety. The novice in such situations should find out where these guards are stationed, and how one contacts them in case of an emergency. It would also be a good idea to introduce yourself to these supportive personnel so that they know that you are a teacher and will recognize you in a crisis situation.

Teacher's unions and faculty committees also work to meet the needs of the teachers. In most schools they have established private facilities which enable the educator to get away from her students during her "free periods" and before and after school in quiet places where she can relax, engage in quiet contemplation or socialize and commiserate with her peers. These facilities include such places as a faculty lounge, library and lunchroom. All of these areas are off-limits to the students and they are the only places in the building where teachers can take off their shoes, smoke cigarettes and have good cries without fear of interruptions from their pupils.

These groups sponsor faculty gatherings such as teas and dinner-dances where the novice can meet her colleagues in a social situation and increase her sphere of friends. She is given the opportunity at these affairs to meet with faculty members she rarely sees in the course of the school day.

Unions establish organizations which give financial assistance to individual instructors. Credit organizations lend money to teachers at low interest rates and with liberal repayment plans. They frequently make arrangements with selected local businessmen to supply cars and appliances to teachers at discount rates. Bookstores and movie theaters often grant reduced rates to teachers too. It would be a good idea to inquire about such arrangements from the businesses you intend to patronize.

While the new teacher should not enter a school system with a "what can you do to make me happy and make my job easier" attitude, she should make every effort to learn all she can about the supportive services which are available to her and her pupils. The reasons for this are obvious. First, the more thoroughly acquainted the educator is with the facilities available for educating her pupils, the infinitely more effective she is going to be in the classroom. Secondly, the greater the use she makes of the programs provided for her benefit, the happier she is going to be in her job and consequently, the more fulfilled she will be as a human being and as a teacher.

Chapter Thirteen

Problems in Education

Teachers contemplating their initial entrances into the classroom are faced with standard, almost traditional, problems. All novices should be aware of the fact that they must establish satisfactory working relationships with peers and students if the educational process is to succeed. Personalities and teaching techniques have to be altered to meet the needs of school programs and pupil abilities. A thorough knowledge of subject matter is vitally important. And finally, the discovery of methods which permit the grading of papers, planning of lessons, teaching of classes and maintaining of personal life within the confines of a day containing only twenty-four hours seems impossible but is essential.

Demands such as these are the obvious practicalities of our educational system for which all realistic novices are usually prepared long before they approach their first student teaching assignments. However, the problems for which most new teachers are not prepared are those which are indigenous to the different kinds of schools in existence in the United States. Rural, inner-city and suburban institutions each present problems which are unique in comparison with each other. The location of the school in which you are employed determines the type of problems with which you will have to cope.

Unfortunately, student teachers and novices are often prone to evidence symptoms of the "grass is greener" syndrome shortly after they have begun to work in the classroom. This disorder has its basis in the feeling that teaching assignments in other areas are infinitely more desirable than the one in which the newcomer is currently employed. For some educators, this dissatisfaction becomes a perpetual problem leading to frequent transfers and constant dissatisfaction with one's job. To offset this problem, the potential teacher would be wise to take as objective a look at future areas of employment as possible before she accepts any permanent position. Obviously, there are desirable as well as undesirable aspects to working in each of three types of school locations or some areas would have no teachers working in them at all. The time to consider the kind of locality in which to seek employment is before you are emotionally and financially committed to a particular situation.

The new teacher should remember that there is no such thing as an ideal teaching assignment. All positions rely on the educator's affinity for her subject matter and her ability to relate well to young people. However, suitability is relative. It depends upon the personality, interests, training and emotional and intellectual needs of the individual. The early years in the classroom are very hectic. Even the novice who has been an outstanding student in college method and theory courses finds herself overwhelmed by the demands made in actual classroom situations. The exhaustion resulting from attempts to adjust to new roles and responsibilities makes it difficult for a person to honestly evaluate the assets and liabilities of the position itself.

Included in this chapter are the major difficulties found in the different types of teaching areas. While it is hoped that each generation of college graduates can make tremendous strides in guiding society to eliminate these problems, it must be remembered that change is an extremely slow process. In addition to working to eradicate those conditions which work contrary to the educational processes, the novice should be prepared to function in the system as it exists. The various hardships against which you will have to work should be considered carefully and weighed against your ability to handle them before any contract is signed.

INNER-CITY SCHOOLS

Research done for the National Association of Secondary School Principals and reported in their January 1971 *Bulletin* concluded that the big cities of this country are in deep trouble educationally. It stated that "recognized until just a few years ago as the home of the very best schools, they now have few of the most successful schools and many of the most problem-ridden." One of the biggest problems teachers have in the inner-city is adjusting to pupils' different sets of values and goals. Since the majority of educators come from middle class environments, they find it difficult to understand the values of their students and capitalize on them to the best advantages of both.

Attendance and punctuality in inner-city schools are notoriously poor. It is not unusual to find fifteen pupils present in a class which has thirty or thirty-five on the roll. The fifteen who are present are not regular attendees so the chances are rather good that they are not the same fifteen who were present the day before. Therefore, the teacher finds it almost impossible to assign, collect or evaluate long-range assignments, or even daily assignments. It is equally difficult to maintain continuity in lesson planning. Classwork should be kept short and not extended into subsequent periods because those who participated in the first half of the lesson will miss the conclusion and vice-versa.

Chronic lateness for class, as well as for school, is a great annoyance. Pupils straggle into the room twenty or thirty minutes after the session has begun. Their entrance disrupts work in progress and they must be given additional instruction to bring them up to date or they will learn nothing for the remainder of the time they are in the room. Often, these students are late because they are just arriving at school or because they have been loitering in halls, lunchrooms or lavatories, leaving for class when it is convenient for them

199

to do so. As long as they arrive sometime during the period they feel that they have fulfilled their attendance obligations. This makes it difficult for the teacher to treat them sympathetically when they do arrive and the ensuing mutual hostility makes learning difficult. The strained relationship fosters further lateness and cutting. The cycle of lateness, inability to fit into work in progress, lack of interest followed by further lateness is self-perpetuating and frustrating.

One of the greatest difficulties with which the educator in an inner-city school is faced is that of alienation. The teacher is an outsider. Not only is she often a resident of another community, but many times is of a different ethnic, racial, social and economic group. In recent years, ghetto-dwellers have become increasingly more suspicious of outsiders. Many residents come from homes which evidence little respect for formal education. This view is understandable when considered in light of the fact that those members of minority groups who have managed to secure a sound education have been discriminated against by employers because of their backgrounds. Thus, many inner-city residents have little respect for formal education. They turn instead to the more practical things they can learn in their home territories. These things include subjects totally foreign to the majority of new teachers such as how to pad holes in shoes with newspapers, how to avoid the rent collector indefinitely, which gangs to avoid, how to catch a rat in a homemade trap, what territory is safe to cross after dark, who peddles dope to the children in the elementary school and which merchants give the correct change and use honest scales.

This lack of appreciation for the school as a worthwhile institution makes communication between parents, students and teachers difficult. Novices are frequently shocked to discover that even though large percentages of their students are failing in the course work, the teachers themselves are the only ones who appear for Parents' Night meetings. Furthermore, few families answer personal summonses from teachers or counselors to come to school to discuss their children's progress or lack of it.

Despite the lack of individual parental interest, new teachers often find that their schools are in turmoil because parents want control of the schools locally. Extensive community involvement in school activities is beneficial because it forces the community to become involved with school problems and take an active interest in school functions. Yet, it causes problems because hiring, firing, promotion and curriculum-planning philosophies are not consistent throughout the school system or even throughout the district. Personalities and individual prejudices can easily interfere with good educational practices.

Inner-city educators are often separated from their students by language barriers and goal differences. Each generation has its own vocabulary which a new teacher must learn and understand if she is to communicate with her classes. While the teacher does not try to make herself "one of the gang" by using or overusing her pupils' slang, she should know enough of it to enable her to interpret what the class is saying to her. This problem of communication and vocabulary differences is even more acute in the inner-cities where the residents have complete vocabularies and intonational patterns which are totally alien to the teacher. This type of problem has found voice in the controversy over "Black English." For a time, some educators advocated the use in the classroom of speech patterns used by black students in their home environments. Trying to deny the existence of such an inner-directed language was deemed ludicrous in the face of its obvious existence. More recently, the popular approach has been one of trying to make the pupils bi-dialectical. Teachers are learning and accepting "Black English" as an effective means of communication within the home community while trying to train students to use the standard English forms necessary for success in the business community.

The goals of ghetto-dwelling youngsters are often as foreign to the teacher as their speech patterns. Even though schools are instruments of "the system" designed to help the individual to conform to and succeed within the confines of established society, inner-city youngsters are programmed to live outside of society. They are geared to trying to "beat the system," not succeeding within it. Some are so worried about getting after-school jobs or trying to avoid the wrath of rival gangs or keeping younger siblings from getting hooked on dope that they can't worry about completing a research assignment on India or going to college in four or five years. Therefore, the teacher must learn to adapt her subject matter to their more immediate goals of physical and economic survival rather than to potential worldly success or the mere joy of learning.

Often, inner-city teachers and students have to become accustomed to the idea of going to school in fear. Those in urban areas frequently admit to being afraid of gang activity. Students skip lunch because they are afraid to go into the lunchroom, refuse to change their clothes for gym because of unsafe locker room conditions, come to school late because they must take a circuitous route to avoid certain "turf," refuse to work in groups containing rival gang members, will not stay after school for conferences because they are safer in crowds and do not have supplies for classwork because they have been extorted from them as they pass through the halls. Such excuses are legitimate more often than they are fraudulent. They should be seriously considered before assigning a punishment for a rule infraction.

Teachers are not free from the problems of protecting personal safety either. Many come to school early so that they can park their cars close to the building. They, too, leave immediately after class to avoid being alone in the building or on the street. They travel in groups in the halls and lock their classrooms when they are working alone during their free periods. Car antennae and vinyl roofs have to be replaced frequently and teachers learn to carry no more than carfare and lunch money in their wallets.

The prevalence of fear of physical harm and loss of personal property is somewhat lessened in many city schools by the presence of police and security guards. Yet, the idea of attending classes and sporting events under the protection of guards tends to have a depressing, stifling influence on the creativity and enthusiasm of both the students and the educators.

Public education, because of its vastness, requires that the student body conform to a wide variety of rules and procedures in order to insure its smooth functioning. When as many as five thousand teen-agers are together for prolonged periods of time, a degree of conformity is necessary to prevent chaos and injury. Following rules and regulations is particularly difficult for the ghetto-dwelling youngster. The inner-city child learns to be independent at an early age. Long before they reach their teens, many girls assume the duties of running households and caring for younger children while parents are employed. Boys frequently substitute as father figures before they are old enough to shave. Because of the absence of adult figures, due either to desertion, neglect or the necessity for long working hours, ghetto home environments are often chaotic. Confusion, noise, dirt and lack of organization are the norm, not the exception. Then, when the school expects students to sit in assigned seats, eat only in specified areas at particular times, wear regulation clothes for gym and raise their hands before speaking, the pupils are unable and unwilling to adjust. They reject these regulations as further proof that the schools are alien representatives of middle-class values which are totally unsuited for meeting their needs.

Ghetto-dwelling youngsters are prone toward physical rather than mental action. The noise and lack of privacy at home prevents them from studying. Doing homework becomes an impossibility. Sitting down to read a book or draw a picture in quiet solitude is never even considered. Their world expects them to react physically. If they do not, they are likely to find themselves in physical danger. To protect their own interests, most take action first and think later. This is a very difficult habit for the newcomer to adjust to. A teacher who affectionately puts a hand on a pupil's shoulder while she is examining his work or touches his arm to direct him to the proper stairway during a fire drill may find that she has an elbow thrust into her stomach before the pupil realizes what he has done. The students act instinctively to protect themselves. The teacher must be extremely careful to avoid any unnecessary physical contact, no matter how well-intentioned it is.

In even the most modern, well-equipped schools, inner-city students lack the proper tools for learning. They have little respect for personal property. New schools are quickly vandalized and covered with graffiti. This reaction is understood when one realizes that few pupils have any possessions which they don't have to share with brothers and sisters or have parents who own any private property. Their homes belong to absentee landlords, and television sets and refrigerators are owned by finance companies. Those who are given books and pencils lose them, forget them on buses or destroy them because they've had no training in caring for or appreciating personal property.

Opportunities for cultural enrichment outside of the classroom are almost nonexistent for the ghetto youngster. Few students, including the more mature group leaders have been further than a few blocks from their own homes. Their entire lives have been spent in the limited areas encompassing their homes and school. Some high school students graduate without ever having been in the downtown area of the city. Difficult as it is for the novice to accept, many inner-city high school students have never ridden buses or subways to go any place except to school and do not know how to read train and bus schedules. Therefore, their experiences and the things to which they can relate are extremely limited. The teacher has to work hard to find things which are meaningful for the student without lowering her expectations or educational goals.

The preceding discussion of inner-city educational difficulties must make the prospect of working in an urban school sound quite dismal. There is a big turnover of staff in urban schools each year. This helps to contribute to the pupils' lack of security and their rejection of teachers as disinterested individuals. Yet, despite this depressing picture, there are numerous points to be made in favor of teaching in an urban area.

Ghetto-dwelling youngsters are extremely aggressive. They have learned from experience that they must work hard to obtain what they want. A teacher who is wise will learn to channel this aggression and determination into worthwhile, profitable learning activities. Once motivated, the pupils will work toward a goal with amazing dedication.

Because of the absence of parental authority figures, inner-city children take direction from other youngsters. This characteristic can be of great service to the teacher who is able to identify the class leaders and gain their cooperation. Her difficulties with disruptive students will diminish considerably once she is able to accomplish this.

Students in these areas have an awareness and realistic approach to life which is lacking in pupils in economically privileged areas. Culturally-different young people represent an untapped resource for change and the improvement of society which the skillful teacher has the opportunity to channel and direct for the good of society.

Large school systems are able to provide supportive services which are not available in suburban or rural districts. Most schools have counselors, medical personnel and therapists in the schools daily. Emergencies and routine problems can be handled immediately rather than once a week as is often the case in small districts. City schools have the benefit of additional funds and staff as a result of federal grants. Student-teacher ratios are substantially lower than in high-status schools. Extensive learning equipment such as television studios, tape recorders, large libraries and teaching machines are also more accessible in urban schools than they are in other areas.

The absence of strict supervision of classroom activities combined with the desperation many administrators feel in city schools permit frequent unbridled experimentation with new techniques and subject matter. The novice is usually at liberty to fulfill herself pedagogically and to satisfy her intellectual curiosity about the feasibility of new techniques or approaches without fear of interference as long as she has taken precautions to protect the safety of her pupils.

Contrary to the situation existing in previous decades, present salaries in large school districts are higher than those in suburban and rural areas. City teachers are freer to join unions and have more supportive personal services available to them than do their counterparts in other locations. In-service courses, paid for by the system, and new teachers' supervisors are available to help the novice adjust to her position. The resources, both medical and cultural, of the big city are available for use by the teacher with her classes and for herself. These civic institutions such as museums, libraries and theaters help to augment the extensive facilities of the school districts and enhance the learning experiences of the students when used wisely by the educator.

The inner-city teacher has an opportunity to make a contribution to the betterment of society beyond that made by other classroom teachers. She has the opportunity to help direct the activities of young people who have been neglected for most of their lives and who will continue to be so unless educated people take an active interest in their development. This is important for the preservation and growth of these individuals as well as for society as a whole. The urban teacher must remember that, for the most part, her pupils are underfed, underclothed, in need of medical or dental attention and lacking in mature, responsible adult-identification figures. The classroom teacher in the inner-city has the

206

opportunity to be a social worker, human relations representative, friend and counselor in addition to her role as an educator. The satisfactions reaped from performing these functions successfully are inestimable. Those educators who can cope with the pressures inherent in urban classrooms will find their careers professionally and emotionally very rewarding.

SUBURBAN SCHOOLS

Potential educators often think of a position in a suburban school as the ideal teaching assignment. Yet, those who are experienced educators reveal that the suburbs are not the havens for teachers that they are often pictured as being. Their problems, while different from those found in the inner-city, are no less acute or disturbing for the novice.

Children residing in what are commonly referred to as "nice" neighborhoods lead very sheltered lives. They are not forced to cope with the realities of poverty, prejudice, deprivation, dirt and hatred. Some refuse to acknowledge that such conditions exist. As their counterparts in the inner-cities, few have contacts with people from other racial and ethnic groups. Many reach maturity experiencing only the "good life" and have little understanding or compassion for the world's problems.

Such one-sided views of life contribute to lacks of imagination and creativity. Suburban students traditionally conform to their parents' or friends' values without questioning or evaluating them. Teachers who try to foster creativity and individuality find, much to their frustration, that students return information on homework and test papers almost exactly as it was given to them in class discussions and lectures. Pupils evidence little proof of individual thought or interpretation. While all young people exhibit a similar need to conform to the dress, values and actions of their peers, suburban youngsters carry this trait to frustrating extremes.

Affluent pupils who have been pampered and catered to by overly-indulgent parents are particularly difficult to handle. Teachers are expected to give them special attention.

They refuse to cooperate for the good of the class and consistently put their personal needs above those of the majority. Often, suburban parents demand special treatment for their children. Obviously such expectations further complicate the teacher's difficulties with her pupils. Students call out in class rather than waiting to be called upon and flagrantly disobey school rules. They fail to meet assignment deadlines and refuse to work to their fullest potentials. Yet, they expect to be rewarded with passing grades nevertheless. Trying to change the behavioral patterns of these pupils is a difficult task.

Equally disturbing to the suburban educator is the lack of respect parents and students hold for teachers. Wealthy pupils flaunt the fact that they dress in more expensive clothes and drive larger cars than their teachers. To them, wealth is a symbol of success. Educators, therefore, are considered failures because their salaries are not comparable to those offered in business and in other professions. Because of their lower financial statuses, teachers' opinions are not accepted as having value. Parents encourage this kind of feeling by remarks about their abilities to "buy and sell that teacher ten times over." Since parents in suburban communities frequently serve on their local school boards, they have more direct control over teachers than do city parents. They exert more pressure over educators' salaries and curriculum choices. Thus, teachers feel more pressured to please parental groups and more stifled in taking punitive or innovative action than they do in large city systems where school boards are not personally or emotionally involved with the activities of a particular school or teacher.

Inner-city teachers are distressed by a lack of parental interest and participation in the educational process. Suburban educators are often hampered by the excessive concern of their pupils' parents. While all parents have the right to expect teachers to interpret or explain grades, test scores and the purposes for assignments, suburban parents tend to be highly critical and very demanding of the personnel in their schools. They have a tendency to reject the idea of student failure and substitute teacher inadequacy in its place. It is not unusual for teachers of college-bound students to be called upon to justify a final average of 88 as opposed to 87 or to explain why she has deviated from the syllabus slightly.

Despite the fact that suburban educators often have the advantage of having modern facilities with which to work, they are stifled in their desires to experiment with new subject matter and teaching techniques. This can be attributed to the severe pressure for the maintenance of high grades. Students feel that admission to a prestigious university is essential. Competition for honors and high places in their graduating classes is very strong. For this reason, parents demand that teachers follow prescribed courses of study very carefully so that students will be prepared to compete in college entrance and scholarship examinations. They fear, and possibly rightfully so, that any deviation or experimentation will have an adverse effect on their test scores. Understandable as this view is, it has a suffocating effect upon the educator's creative and innovative desires.

This severe pressure for academic achievement, while acting as a motivational force for hard work and learning, exerts a depressing influence upon original thought. Students are afraid to exhibit independent ideas for fear that any diversion from established or previously-expressed concepts will result in grade penalties. Questions are answered the way pupils think the teacher wants them answered rather than the way the students believe they should be answered. Youngsters are reluctant to commit themselves to a point of view in opinion questions. Open expression of ideas occurs less frequently than in urban classrooms. Homework and test papers are turned in quoting information cited in class discussions almost verbatim.

Yet, the stress on academic achievement has its beneficial aspects in that it leads to a great professional challenge for the teacher. In city secondary schools many educators express the opinion that their years of college training in subject matter go to waste because they devote most of their class-room time to the discussion of elementary skills such as simple addition or letter writing. Suburban teachers, to the contrary, spend hours researching and preparing lessons and lectures which keep up with the needs of their brighter pupils. Urban teachers are challenged to find ways to make simple skills interesting for their mature and worldly pupils. Suburban educators have to find enough time to research their subjects thoroughly enough to keep ahead of the class. This is particularly difficult for a novice who must do this extensive lesson preparation in addition to becoming accustomed to the routine requirements of her assignment. Pupils in these areas are highly-motivated, have good reference resources at home, have been exposed to cultural elements and are frequently more widely-traveled than their teachers.

Suburban students are well-fed youngsters who come from families which value education and take an interest in the quality of the school. Teachers in these schools are constantly being challenged by their pupils and colleagues. They grow intellectually as a result of their relationships with their classes. Working conditions are pleasant, safe and clean.

Stability exists in the working conditions because the teacher turnover rate is relatively low and the student dropout rate is small. Yet, they must cope with the pressures of students with strong cultural backgrounds who are overly motivated to achieve high grades. Satisfactory relationships have to be established with parents who pressure teachers and students excessively to assure that excellence is achieved. The impression of teachers as underpaid workers who cannot meet the competition of big business must be eradicated.

The problem of lack of respect is particularly acute for male teachers. Suburban youngsters share the problem of the lack of male-identification figures with inner-city children. Middle and upper-class fathers spend many hours working toward success in the business and professional worlds. They are as absent from their homes as those fathers who have literally deserted their families. Male pupils are particularly demanding of their male teachers because they expect them to fill the father-figure void. Yet, they reject them at the same time because they are not the affluent professionals their fathers are trying to be.

Today, suburban educators generally earn less than those in the inner-city. This has not always been true. Recently, however, cities have tried to induce more qualified teachers into their areas by raising salaries and hiring para-professionals to help teachers with their clerical and supervisory duties. Strong unions in urban areas have also helped to bring about this disparity. Those employed in suburban areas contend, however, that the more pleasant working conditions compensate for the salary differences.

Before accepting a teaching position, the potential educator should consider her own personality, emotional and financial needs. These should be compared with the rewards and difficulties found in suburban and urban areas. It is true that a person who truly likes working with young people and is enthusiastic about her subject matter can be successful in any location. Still, the greater the satisfaction the individual feels in her assignment, the more effective she will be.

RURAL SCHOOLS

All children need and deserve a superior education. However, some educators believe that quality education in rural areas is even more vital than it is in other areas. The schools in isolated areas must supply all of the cultural elements to which the students are exposed. Residents of the poorest ghettos have access to television sets, magazines, radios, newspapers, theaters and other intellectually-stimulating sources. True, these are not always used to their best advantages or even for the purposes for which they were originally intended. Yet, they are present in the pupil's environments and some constructive effects are bound to rub off despite, or in spite of, the students' resistance. In rural areas, these creative thought stimulants are virtually nonexistent. The school is called upon to fill the total cultural void as well as performing all the routine educational functions.

It is difficult for people, most of whom are raised in or near populated areas, to imagine the condition of rural schools. School districts exist which are so small that one centrally-located school of five hundred children serves all the pupils in grades kindergarten through twelve. Despite this, the National Association of Secondary School Principals estimates that 31% of this country's youth are currently enrolled in rural schools.

Roster planners are frequently faced with the difficult decision of whether to conduct classes of four or five learners in the third year of a course or not to have it at all. Often, teachers in one subject area will have as many as five or six different classes daily each requiring a separate preparation. Teachers' organizations in more highly-populated locations have made great strides in eliminating this problem, but in rural areas it is still an educational reality.

The main problems of rural education can be summed up in a single word "lack." There is a lack of medical and social services in rural districts. Many communities have no doctors or dentists permanently located within fifty miles of their homes. Social services are completely unavailable. This is as much of an inconvenience for the teacher as it is for the student. Sickly students are poor learners for obvious reasons. Teachers are naturally concerned about the effect of the absence of emergency and routine medical services for themselves, their families and their students. This is a particularly acute problem for teachers with families and for those pupils with chronic illnesses requiring regular professional supervision and treatment.

Employees in rural areas should be prepared for the fact that living conditions will be inferior to those in other locations. Sanitary conditions are substandard and modern facilities such as air-conditioning, washing machines, telephones and, often, indoor plumbing are not available. The physical dwellings themselves are frequently antiquated, dilapidated and poorly heated. The school buildings are no exception to this.

Homes in these communities are clustered together in small groups with great distances existing between each cluster and a few isolated individuals living in between. This gives the teacher little opportunity for privacy. In densely populated areas, it is not unusual for teachers to live fifteen or twenty miles away from their schools. Rural educators must live close to their schools and in the same communities as their pupils. This gives them few chances for private lives. On the other hand, it gives them a chance to become a part of the community in which they are working which is denied to their urban counterparts. They are able to really get to know and understand the families with which they are working and establish more meaningful relationships than teachers in impersonal situations can do.

Professionally, rural education presents numerous hardships for the educator and especially for the novice. Rural schools report high staff turnovers. There are few experienced teachers for the newcomer to emulate or consult for advice. Few districts can afford to hire trained professional supervisors to help new employees adjust to their positions.

Teachers are hampered in their own intellectual development by a lack of professional stimulation and an absence of cultural elements. There are no professional meetings, discussion groups or university seminars gathering close enough for the teacher to attend with any regularity. It is almost impossible for a person to continue her education while employed in a rural district.

The rural educator must be prepared to cope with many professional frustrations. In addition to lower salaries, she must be ready to attempt to function with minimal, often nonexistent, facilities and funds. Much of what she has learned in college training courses about innovations in education and new techniques will be useless because of the rudimentary facilities and absence of supplies and teaching aids. She finds herself doubling as a magician, trying to invent articles to substitute for the books and instruments she needs but does not have. She learns to share resources with seven or eight area schools. This means that a library lesson begun on Tuesday cannot be continued until the following Tuesday when the mobile library returns to her school.

The limited size of school populations puts many restrictions upon curriculum offerings. A teacher might not be able to introduce a new course for which she has been specially trained such as black literature, space science or Hebrew because there are too few demands for it. This is disturbing on both a professional and a personal level. She cannot fulfill the needs of the few students she discovers who would profit from her knowledge and she is prevented from using her specialized skills.

Factors mentioned earlier such as high staff turnovers, lack of sufficient funds and facilities, absences of professional stimulation and limited choices of course offerings contribute to substandard curriculum quality. This is disturbing for all dedicated educators, but for the novice it is particularly difficult to accept. Many recently-learned approaches to education are unusable.

Curriculum development is particularly difficult in rural areas. Jobs for youngsters in unskilled positions are almost nonexistent. Few have the funds or the desire to go on to post-high school training. Teachers must prepare their students to function in the outside world. Studies indicate that most rural youngsters leave their home communities as soon as they reach maturity. Many run away even before then. This means that educators have to prepare their charges to function in a world totally different from their own. This task is complicated by the fact that country dwellers are traditionally suspicious of outsiders and "foreign ways" of doing things. Furthermore, because youngsters have not been exposed to the outside world, they have no frames of reference upon which to base their studies. This makes communication between teacher and class and between teacher and the community difficult.

The prospect of accepting employment in rural areas seems dismal on initial examination. Yet, the educator in such communities has opportunities for personal fulfillment which are denied to personnel in other locations. She can work with students on individual levels which are totally impossible in larger school districts. The progress of youngsters through their educational careers and often even longer can be followed. This leads to a feeling of satisfaction which is lost in the anonymity of densely-populated areas.

Rural educators become "all things to all people." They accomplish infinitely more than teaching mathematics or science. They become actively involved in community problems. They teach sanitation, give child-rearing and family-planning advice, counsel disturbed individuals and double as civic servants. The absence of the variety of pressures which are normally found in other school situations enables teachers to concentrate on the business of education without worrying about the activities of the school board, union or local gangs.

Teachers in rural areas carry tremendous responsibilities, but they can also become satisfied, stimulated individuals. They have the opportunity to perform services to numbers far greater than those students and community residents with whom they work directly. They are enabled to help the entire country by uplifting the standards of people who have been virtually forgotten or ignored by the bulk of society. Rural educators work to help residents of neglected communities help themselves to find meaningful and satisfying lives. In the process, they fulfill themselves as teachers and as human beings.

Chapter Fourteen

Innovations in Education

Education is a dynamic, constantly-changing field. Innovative techniques are introduced into the classroom as soon and as often as the creative educator conceives of ways to improve old methods and brings about the necessary provisions for the implementation of new approaches. Some innovative approaches prove impractical or unsuccessful and are quickly dropped in favor of newer or older more reliable methods. Others, however, which give evidence of being satisfactory teaching devices are adopted by other teachers and eventually by entire school systems.

Basically inventive approaches to education come from two major sources; the imaginations and experiences of individual classroom teachers and administrators and from the research and studies of educational theorists, students and professors. Since the launching of the first Sputnik by the Russians in the 1950s, the concern for education has soared tremendously. In the past two decades, a greater concentration of creative power and financial resources has been expended in the area of educational research than perhaps that which occurred in all the previous years of public education in this country.

What follows here is a summary of some of the more recent approaches to teaching which have proven successful in classrooms in urban, suburban and rural areas. As the need arises, the new teacher would be wise to try to adapt some of these techniques to her own classroom situation, always keeping in mind the abilities of her students, the school's physical plant and resources and her own talents, capabilities and interests. She may find that some of these "innovative approaches" are already commonplace practices in her school while others will be impractical for a variety of reasons.

The bulk of today's creative efforts are being directed primarily toward meeting the needs of the individual and preparing him to function in the complexities of modern society. This is a Gargantuan task when one realizes that it must be accomplished within the confines of a broad educational system dedicated to accommodating the need of the entire educable population of an entire country. The second educational drive is aimed at trying to help the many different members of society to communicate and interrelate with each other. Improving human relations and providing for individual differences in learning are the main concerns of today's educational planners.

HUMAN RELATIONS

More than at any other time in our history, today's schools are taking on the difficult challenge of trying to teach people to get along with each other. Theoretical courses in understanding people of foreign lands have been part of secondary school curriculums for many years. Recently, however, schools have been focusing their efforts on bringing the diverse cultural, racial and ethnic elements of this nation's population closer together.

Community Relations: One of the more successful programs for improving community relations involves parent-to-parent, parent-to-pupil, pupil-to-pupil, and neighbor-to-school representative discussions and forums at informal breakfasts, "koffee klatches," teas and evening meetings. Such gatherings take place in the school, at the homes of faculty members or community leaders and in churches, fire stations or other local meeting places. These gatherings provide opportunities for the school and the community to openly and informally discuss complaints, rumors and methods for meeting each other's needs and solving mutual problems.

These sessions not only foster understanding and cooperation in particularly hostile, tense situations, but also contribute to the social awareness and growth of both groups by providing forums for meaningful communication. Meetings of this type are especially useful in areas in which racial tensions exist or where the school population is very diverse culturally, ethnically or racially. Even in situations where problems of this nature are minimal, a close cooperation between the school and the surrounding community can only serve to work to the advantage of both sectors. An opportunity for open exchanges of opinions and points of view is provided by these relaxed, honest interchanges.

Exchange Programs: Exchange programs with institutions in foreign countries are long-established practices. Most large secondary schools have two or three students a year who come to them from foreign countries in exchange for members of the student body who live away from home for a similar length of time. Both sets of students traditionally live with members of the student body of the host school during their stay in the foreign country.

Recently, educators have become shockingly aware of the fact that the differences between rural and urban, private and public, and urban and suburban schools are almost as great, if not greater, than those existing between American schools and foreign institutions. It has become obvious that suburban dwellers cannot run away from the problems of the inner cities. In the future, urban and suburban areas must find ways to cooperate in the sharing of revenue, facilities and experiences. Realizing this, schools in diverse areas are beginning to work together to establish exchange programs involving teachers and students.

In some programs, teachers trade classes for a semester or an entire year. This exposes classes to new teaching techniques and points of view. It enables educators to learn how schools in areas different from their own function. They meet other professionals and share ideas and approaches. They are also forced to face challenges from students with different values, backgrounds and abilities. This forces them to adapt their teaching methods to meet their new students' needs and they find that they learn as much from their pupils as they are able to teach them. Teachers grow pedagogically as well as socially.

In other exchange situations, individual students, class officers and entire classes attend schools and visit homes in different areas for periods ranging from one day to one semester. This increases understanding, sharing of information and resources, and cooperation between the groups involved. Sports competitions are arranged. Facilities such as exhibitions and teaching machines are shared. Letters are often exchanged. In many instances, tensions between rival areas are alleviated and understanding is increased.

Home-Community Coordinators: Increasing numbers of schools, particularly those in inner-city areas, are employing nonprofessional personnel to work in the schools to help cement and improve relationships between the school and its surrounding community. These coordinators must be residents of the districts in which the school is located. In most cases, they are parents of children attending the school. No formal education or training is required. Their most important attribute is the ability to relate well to people. Main functions include arranging meetings between parents and faculty members, visiting homes of difficult students or potential dropouts, offsetting the spread of rumors, trying to prevent tensions, and setting up programs involving the sharing of school-community resources such as gymnasiums, auditoriums, pools and recreation areas. The coordinators help to arrange for guest speakers from the community to come into the school to confer with parent and student groups. They work with organizations such as the Opportunities Industrialization Center (OIC), Interested Negroes (IN) and the Young Lords, a Puerto Rican self-help organization to help alleviate problems in the school and surrounding communities.

Parent Workshops: Conferences and training workshops are being set up with school principals, teachers and specialists to teach parents how to help children improve their skills in subject areas such as mathematics, reading, science and creative writing. As originally conceived, the main purpose of programs of this type was to help compensate youngsters from poverty areas for the lack of the intellectual stimulation usually found in the home environments of more affluent students. The basis for programs of this type is the belief that inner-city parents want to help their failing children but do not know how to do so effectively. Therefore, most of them turn their efforts toward nagging students to study harder. Little constructive assistance is given, due to a lack of training rather than a lack of concern as some outsiders tend to believe. Parental nagging, in place of constructive help, only serves to reenforce negative feelings toward education.

Programs designed to teach parents how to help pupils have many benefits. The most obvious, of course, is that of improving the quality of student learning. Secondly, it helps to bring the school and home closer together. Each sector is prevented from criticizing or blaming the other for student failures to achieve. Further, working with their own children brings parents and children closer together in a more meaningful relationship. Parents who attempt to assist in the education of their youngsters are less critical of what they previously deemed the teachers' failures to educate their students to the fullest extent desirable. Parents become less suspicious of the school as an alien influence in the lives of their families when they are made a part of the educational process. Occasionally these programs develop into large-scale tutoring programs and volunteer teachers' assistants are trained.

Ethnic Education: Guest speakers and courses are presented to the student body and parental groups to make them aware of the differences and attributes of the diverse groups

221

residing in and near their home territories. Difficult as it may be for an urban dweller to realize, many pupils graduate from secondary schools in suburban or rural locations, just a few miles from large cities, without ever encountering a Puerto Rican or Negro in any other than an employer-employee relationship. Those living in inner-city areas frequently do not communicate with those of other ethnic backgrounds except in the gang-war arenas or in the darker corridors of the school. In such instances, the communication is always physical rather than social.

Guest speakers, research assignments, museum trips and courses in black, Indian, and Puerto Rican history and racial understanding are typical of programs designed to foster understanding and communication between hostile groups.

Community Curriculum Planning: School systems are working toward increased community involvement in the direction and planning of school activities. Parental groups meet with teachers to review curricula materials and goals. Then they make recommendations for additional instruction, revisions and activities in each of the grades and subject areas. After reviewing the suggestions of the parent-teacher group, the total faculty and curriculum specialists prepare suggestions which eventually are examined by the parent-teacher committee. Finally, ideas are worked up into permanent usable forms.

Evening Meetings: To accommodate the large numbers of working parents who cannot meet with teachers during the day, schools are establishing evening conference hours. These sessions, usually held once a week, enable parents to meet with teachers, counselors and administrators to discuss students' problems and methods of overcoming them. Evening meetings help both the school and the community by showing the parents that the school and its teachers are interested enough in helping the pupils to achieve their fullest potentials that they are willing to adjust schedules to accommodate the needs of employed parents. The greatest benefit, however, is that of enabling parents of troubled or troublesome youngsters to meet with professionals to try to solve student difficulties.

Home Visits: Teachers, working in teams or pairs, have been making "house calls" to homes of problem students. They visit the homes of students who have been severe discipline problems, who are potential dropouts or who have actually dropped out of school. Discussions on a private, personal level with parents and students often help to solve problems previously ignored or deemed unsolvable.

IMPROVING INSTRUCTION

While most segments of the economy are refining production methods to meet the needs of the masses, the educational community is concentrating its efforts on trying to meet the needs of the individual. This is an extremely difficult task because of the vast numbers of young people enrolled in secondary schools combined with the general lack of funds available for additional teachers, specialists, classrooms and facilities. To compensate for the shortage of educators and equipment without compromising educational quality, is a difficult thing to achieve. Innovative programs calling for the use of a variety of teaching machines, nonprofessional assistants, the sharing of equipment and resources and new approaches to teaching have been the most recent answers to the problem. The basic aim of modern education is to discover the particular educational requirements of each student on the intellectual, social and emotional levels and to use all of the academic, civic and social resources available to help each student reach his fullest potential.

Mini-Unit Courses: The criteria for the selection of these brief courses is relevancy. They are usually scheduled during study periods, lunch periods, before and after school, or for a week or two while regular classes are in suspension. A popular time for the latter is at the end of the term when the final grades have been recorded and textbooks collected. Attendance in these courses is often on a voluntary basis. Grades are assigned on a pass-fail basis and are not averaged into the students' cumulative records.

The pupils take an active role in planning these courses by suggesting subjects or selecting them from lists provided by the faculty. Enrichment courses include subjects such as criminology, dramatics, public speaking, Viet Nam, minority groups in America, cartooning and creative writing. Interest courses are typified in units such as ham radio, charm and personality, gourmet cooking, the automobile, bridge, carpentry and chess.

Mini-Unit courses stimulate the teacher as much as they arouse the pupil. The professional and personal interests of the teachers are used to their fullest potentials. Community resource personnel can also be called upon to participate in this program.

Flexible Modular Scheduling: This approach to instruction is founded upon a logical concept which occurred to teachers and students quite a few years ago but which was not converted into a workable form until recently. Educators and their pupils have long been aware of the fact that fitting all subjects into equal blocks of time was not a sensible practice because all subjects and skills do not require an equal amount of time for study. Therefore, trying to teach art, reading, Spanish, chemistry and all other subjects in forty-five minute periods or in multiples thereof is impractical. Student attention spans and the amount of time required to learn a skill vary from subject to subject. Flexible modular scheduling tries to alleviate this problem by scheduling courses into class periods of varying lengths to enable the time allotted to coincide with the amount of time needed to cover the lesson thoroughly.

This type of course planning presents the obvious problem of what is to be done with students who have finished a one-hour tennis lesson while others are in a seventy-five minute chemistry laboratory and still others are sculpturing in a two-hour art program. The solution is found in the form of the *Instructional Media Center.*

Instructional Media Center (IMC): The IMC is a vast audio-visual area in which students have the opportunity to engage in independent study and research. Subject matter teachers give students direction in using the facility but freedom of inquiry and research is essential. The ideally-equipped IMC contains viewing rooms and television studios in which pupils can put scripts they have written onto video-tape for replay and discussion. It contains cable television and radios with headphones for private listening. There are dark rooms for developing photos and sound-proof reading rooms with typewriters and record players. Reference texts and paperback books are also essential to a well-equipped IMC.

Other study areas in the IMC emphasize the graphic arts. They contain materials for creating posters, bulletin boards, slides, drawings, graphs and transparencies. Creative thought is further stimulated by displays of photographs, slides, paintings and collages.

Newer schools are being built with areas specifically designed to accommodate Instructional Media Centers. Large areas of the building, and often entire floors, are designed for listening booths, study cubicles, research areas and display rooms. However, in older buildings, a few empty rooms can be converted for use as a Center.

The facilities of the IMC are usually cared for by non-professionals. This frees teachers to work individually with students and to guide them to select projects suited to their talents and capabilities. As in the other innovative programs achieving popularity today, the use of the Instructional Media Center places a large share of the educational burden upon the student himself. Pupils are enabled to explore their skills to their fullest potential without the pressures of "assigned" chores. Many discover that they enjoy learning and develop interests of which they had not been previously aware.

Television: The use of television to supplement learning experiences in schools is not new. However, the extent and the manner in which it is being used currently are new.

A Neilsen study reported recently that television viewing in the average home today amounts to six hours a day. In 1954, the average had been three hours and thirty minutes and a little more than five hours in 1962. To capitalize on this ever-increasing fascination with television, schools are taping programs broadcasted during after-school hours and replaying them when classes are in session.

Closed-circuit television is being used to transmit courses broadcasted from universities and centrally-located high schools in rural areas. This helps to compensate for an absence of sufficient course offerings in small schools. It is also used to tape productions of student-produced plays and dramatic club projects for later critical evaluation by the pupils.

New Courses: In response to the demand for relevancy in education, many secondary schools are introducing courses designed to help the individual improve himself and his environment. These courses are being woven into the regular programs of study with credit being given toward fulfilling graduation requirements. Such additions include courses in philosophy, the humanities and environmental studies which aim toward fostering growth and self-improvement as a result of self-examination.

One new approach to relevant education is called "affective education." This program attempts to get students involved in taking an active part in community problems. Teachers, students and community representatives work together to determine what needs to be done and how the students can help to accomplish the necessary tasks in a manner which will be meaningful to them educationally. In a program of this sort, students are guided to see a direct relationship between what they are learning and how their acquired skills can be used to improve their lives and the lives of those around them.

Schools in rural areas are using the affective education approach in the establishment of environmental centers. Students learn to care for forests, experiment with soil conservation, engage in ecological studies, environmental improvement and landscaping.

Computer education has become popular in many urban and suburban schools. Students work on computers located in the schools or in nearby business establishments. They study computers' functions, their language, programming, care and future. Career opportunities in computers are also discussed.

Independent testing organizations have found that urban youngsters in the inner cities read at grade levels which are several steps below their chronological ages. Conventional attempts to raise reading abilities have failed. Several schools have tried to rectify this situation by converting classrooms into Reading Skills Centers. These centers are used by low-achievers in reading who have failed to improve within the traditional classroom situation. Specially-trained teachers and volunteers work with students on an individual basis on all components of a traditional reading program including word-recognition, phonics, comprehension and motivation. These centers contain special reading textbooks, tapes, listening centers and record players. All materials are specially designed to stimulate the underachiever.

With the aid of federal, local and private funds, many school districts are engaging in intensive and extensive motivational and enrichment programs. These programs are designed to broaden the cultural experiences of under-achieving and culturally-deprived youngsters. Often, these programs are directed by nonteaching personnel who arrange for tickets and transportation for pupils to extracurricular events. Enrichment courses are offered, frequently without credit or charge, during the summer or after the regular school hours. These courses are structured to fill a void which seems to exist in the home environments of some culturally-deprived students who evidence a potential for enrichment despite their previous lack of exposure to intellectual stimulation. Students are chosen for participation in this program on the basis of teacher recommendations, accumulated standardized test scores and the results of specialized aptitude tests. Tutoring programs for remedial and advanced work are necessary if the program is to achieve its avowed purpose of uplifting the standards and abilities of pupils.

Some progressive high schools are following the recent example set by universities in their attempts to de-emphasize the importance of grades and encourage the enjoyment of learning for its own sake. To accomplish this, increasing numbers of courses are being offered on a pass-fail basis. This encourages pupils to elect to take courses such as mathematics and science without being fearful of facing grade penalties for low aptitudes in these areas.

"Vestibule Classes": In previous decades, disruptive students were sent to detention rooms by teachers who could not handle them within the regular classroom situation. There they were "kept" for indefinite periods of time until their temporary guardians, who were usually the strongest males in the school, tired of them and sent them back to their classrooms. This system enabled subject matter teachers to continue instruction with the cooperative pupils while the disruptive ones were prevented from causing any trouble. While learning progressed in the classroom, the outcasts traditionally sat with their hands folded and their minds closed, making no academic or social progress.

Some schools have tried to correct this situation by creating what in Philadelphia are called "Vestibule Classes," so called because the classes meet in areas outside the classroom. These special classes concentrate on teaching the disruptive student (rather than "keeping" him) to adapt to the educational system's standards of good deportment. Conformity to those values which are necessary for success in the business world are stressed. To achieve an understanding of these requirements, an attempt is made to make the student aware of the conditions existing in his world and the worlds with which he must eventually cope. Basically, the curriculum, which is taught to all grade levels, is based upon the development of good attendance patterns in school, the

228

growth of honesty and trust among one's peers, social awareness, the desirability of furthering one's education, good
character and citizenship, orderly methods of doing chores
and the importance of being punctual at school, home and
on the job.

Length of participation in this course is based upon the
teacher's evaluation of the pupil's development. When the
vestibule teacher feels that a student is ready to return to
his regular classroom, he discusses the decision with guidance
personnel and the pupil's subject matter teacher. Based upon
a consensus of their opinions, the student returns to his class
whenever it is deemed that he is ready to do so.

Advanced Placement Courses: To meet the needs of the
superior student, high schools are including advanced placement courses in the curricula. These programs enable students to do college-level work while still in high school.
Qualified personnel are usually on staff in large high schools
to teach these courses with direction from local colleges. In
rural areas, where suitable instructors are rarely available,
schools use taped lectures and study guides, courses by tele-
phone and inter-coms accompanied by slides and after-school
seminars at meeting places convenient to several area secondary schools and a local college or university. Some universities serving rural areas are offering correspondence
courses to high school students who are unable to meet personally with instructors of college-level courses in their home
towns.

Magnet Schools and Open Classrooms: The magnet school
and open-classroom concepts are achieving increasing popularity in highly populated locations. In the magnet school
program, one area high school is selected to specialize in a
specific subject area. The most qualified teachers, latest textbooks and modern facilities are made available in these
specialized schools. Qualified, interested students from all
parts of the city are invited to attend the school which meets
their special needs and abilities. This is contrary to the neighborhood school concept because students are enrolled from

all parts of the district in addition to those residing in the community immediately surrounding the building. Traditional programs also are given in the magnet schools for the neighborhood youngsters. In addition to improving instruction and catering to the talents of the individual, schools of this type have an added advantage of helping to foster integration. Integration is encouraged because pupils come from all sections of the city to participate in the intensive training program and, thus, there is a blending of diverse ethnic and racial groups.

The open classroom, as typified in Philadelphia's Parkway School, makes full use of a community's cultural resources. Admission to such schools is limited so that individual attention can be given to developing the pupils' full intellectual and social potentials. Small classes make it relatively easy for groups to move from one location to another. Classes are held in museums, scientific institutes, business establishments, zoos, parks, court houses, and any other available institutions of scientific, artistic or educational value. Many of these programs are financed jointly by city and suburban school districts. This cooperation also serves the cause of human relations by bringing together inner-city and suburban youngsters for study and meaningful communication.

Rural Innovations: Rural areas have tried to compensate for the lack of facilities in their schools by cooperating with surrounding locations to invest in mobile equipment. Mobile guidance laboratories, filled with career information, testing materials, space for filing student records and a counseling corner are being used in some areas. The counselor visits each school in the district on a regular basis. Traveling in vans of this type represents an improvement over traveling in a car because the counselor is able to bring all the materials she needs with her in an orderly, easily-accessible fashion.

In locations which require students to spend long periods of time riding to and from schools, buses are being equipped with electronic devices to turn them into mobile language laboratories with head phones and taped lessons. This equipment is used while traveling to and from school and on trips to special events. Students take turns using the "audiobus" on a rotating schedule. Often, special events and programs are also taped for use by students whose schedules conflict with the actual presentation of the program.

Remote areas of Alaska are solving the problem of the absence of teachers on a regular basis by flying teachers into villages by helicopter on a rotating schedule. One subject matter teacher comes at a time and instructs all the community children in the different grade levels of her subject. For example, the mathematics teacher arrives on Monday. She covers a week's work in mathematics with all the educable children in the village. When the history teacher is delivered by the helicopter on Tuesday, the mathematics teacher is picked up and taken to another community. This type of teacher-rotation schedule continues through a five-day week. Eventually all major subject areas are covered. Teachers' aides, who are specially-trained residents of the village, help to keep continuity by reviewing work and supervising studies in the interim periods.

Individualizing Instruction: A greater concentration of financial and intellectual resources is being directed toward solving the problem of individualizing instruction than is being expended on any other educational challenge. A variety of solutions, involving varying degrees of teacher-retraining programs, financial investments and curricula revisions, are being tried throughout the country.

The Independent Study Program is a learning situation in which students and teachers meet individually to establish goals, research topics, approaches and deadlines for completed projects. Time periods are provided in the pupils' schedules to enable them to do research in the school library and with outside facilities. In some programs of this type students select their own research advisors and in others they are assigned to specific teachers for guidance. Whichever situation prevails, students are guided to select a project suited to the students' individual interests, talents and abilities.

Schools which are understaffed or overpopulated have been experimenting with Individualized Progress Programs. Students are given lists of the course requirements, materials, outlines and assignments at the beginning of the semester. They then proceed to work at their own rates of speed with assistance and guidance from the teacher as it is needed. Schools using this approach have found that their learners generally complete more than the required course work and appear highly motivated to see how much they can accomplish within the allotted time period.

Without question, the most widely accepted, enthusiastically received new approach to individualizing instruction is the Individually Prescribed Instruction Program (IPI). This program was developed in a public elementary school in a suburban district of Pittsburgh, Pennsylvania. It proved to be so successful and the response from educators all over the country was so enthusiastic that plans are now underway in virtually every major school district to adapt forms of the IPI at both the elementary and secondary school levels.

The basis of the IPI is relatively simple, but its effectiveness is contingent upon complex behind-the-scenes planning and organization. The guiding principle of this program is that instruction must be aimed at fulfilling the needs and abilities of every pupil individually. This is accomplished through the use of "prescriptions" containing very specific directions, activities and materials written by the teacher for each pupil in her class. In order to write meaningful prescriptions, the educator must first make detailed provisions for the diagnosis of student skills and abilities. A constant check on the pupils' progress must also be maintained if the subsequent prescriptions are to be meaningful.

The IPI program depends heavily upon the teacher. Her role is very different from that of the leader in a traditional classroom. There is little, if any, time spent in group lecture or discussion situations. Most of the teacher's efforts are devoted to evaluating the pupil's records, diagnosing his needs and writing the specific individual learning prescriptions for each student. The largest segments of her time are spent helping individual learners, evaluating, securing and adapting materials and procedures to fulfill the requirements of the prescriptions and making future plans for each learner.

The major duties of the instructor in an IPI learning situation are:

1. Diagnose pupil strengths and weaknesses on the basis of background information, placement test results and pre-test scores.
2. Prepare the initial prescriptions including the learning chores based on completing self-instructional work sheets, group instruction, use of audio-visual equipment or specialized tutoring. Included in these prescriptions are testing devices called Curriculum-Embedded Tests which measure the amount of pupil comprehension of a desired skill and his progress toward achieving an objective or goal.
3. Analyze individual progress through a review of the completed worksheets, the amount of time spent finishing the task and the results of the Curriculum-Embedded Tests.
4. Act as a guide or directional source by explaining difficult directions, assisting poor or nonreaders in carrying out assignments, leading small group instruction, encouraging peer tutoring, working with individual pupils, conducting large group evaluations and giving oral check-ups.
5. Writing the next prescriptions for students who are ready for them.
6. Administering written and oral unit tests and post-tests.
7. Evaluating results of class performance to determine student achievement as well as the success of the approach.

As in many of the other programs emphasizing individualized instruction, student self-direction is of the utmost importance in achieving meaningful learning. The learner is expected to gather the learning equipment required by his personalized prescription and to proceed to work independently. He is required to cope with the learning chores assigned to him before asking the teacher's help. He is en-

couraged to evaluate his own progress and to actively participate in the decision as to whether he has learned enough of
the unit to prepare him to take the post-unit test which, if
passed successfully, will enable him to proceed to the next
lesson.

The student is always permitted and encouraged to use
any supplementary materials he feels he needs to help him
master a skill. This freedom of choice and emphasis on self-
direction is based upon two educational theories. First, the
more individualized the instruction, the more meaningful
it will be for the learner and consequently the greater the
degree of learning that occurs. Second, because IPI places
the responsibility for learning directly upon the student himself, he develops competency in self-direction. The quality
of assuming the responsibility for one's own actions or lack
of them prepares the individual to be an autonomous problem-
solver in response to those experiences he will encounter in
his mature roles of citizen, parent and employee. Such a
skill trains him to meet the unexpected demands and pressures he will be forced to face as an adult.

A conversion to an IPI system involves a retraining of
teachers and students to prepare them to use this different
approach to education to its best advantage. It also involves
additional funds to finance supportive personnel and teaching
equipment. Teacher aides are vitally important to help
teachers with the distribution and care of materials and with
the grading of diagnostic and pre- and post-test results. The
assumption of the latter responsibility by supportive personnel is extremely important because it frees the teacher
to write the extensive prescriptions required for each pupil.
If assistants cannot be hired and volunteers cannot be obtained, students can be called upon to grade some of their
own tests.

While the response to IPI has been overwhelmingly
favorable in the many locations in which it is currently in
practice, several problems still have to be worked out. One
of these involves the assignment of report card grades. No

satisfactory answer to the problem of how to determine what grade to assign for the work accomplished has yet been found.

Another problem involves the pressures on the teacher to create individual prescriptions for each student. This difficulty is somewhat alleviated by the fact that the IPI program minimizes the importance of homework and emphasizes the necessity for teacher aides to grade students' work. Thus, the teacher has additional time to devote to the writing of the required prescriptions.

Finally, funds must be available to provide in-service programs to retrain teachers to carry out the requirements of the IPI system and storage areas must be purchased to house completed work, advance prescriptions and supplementary teaching devices.

Despite the difficulties presented by a conversion to IPI, most educational authorities and classroom teachers feel that the time and financial investments are compensatory for the additional learning accrued. It is felt by local educators and the federal education representatives who have reviewed the program that the IPI is the most practical answer we have to adapting the schools to the needs of the different, unique individuals who attend them. Schools across the United States are adapting the IPI program with the assistance of the twenty United States Office of Education regional educational laboratories. The USOE attempts to export what they deem to be effective innovations into the nation's schools as quickly as possible in an attempt to reduce the wide gap between the discovery of better means of education and the actuality of getting them into practice in a significant number of classrooms.

The enthusiasm for IPI appears to be nationwide with both educational theorists and classroom teachers. It is felt that the approach has provided a significant advancement into the difficult problem of providing for the individual needs of each student within the confines of an educational system which must encompass the bulk of the educable population.

CONCLUSION

Course content, teaching methods and theories of effective education will continue to change as long as humanity and the needs of society are volatile. This presents a great challenge to the dedicated educator. She must learn to identify the needs, personal as well as intellectual, of her charges. Then she has to discover techniques within the confines of her own abilities, her school district's facilities and philosophies, the current research of educational theorists and the changing problems of society to satisfy her pupils' educational requirements. It is a difficult, almost overwhelming task, but one which if successfully accomplished can lead to tremendous personal satisfaction and enrichment and a contribution to the good of society.

Chapter Fifteen

Problems for Consideration

No matter how many times the prospective educator has read *Blackboard Jungle* or how vivid her imagination is, the new teacher cannot begin to imagine the magnitude or variety of the problems she will face during her first years in the classroom. In the classroom, when a teacher under pressure is confronted with a particularly frustrating or emotionally-charged situation, she is apt to do something in confusion or in a rage which she will regret moments after she has done it. Decisions made in times of anger, fear or confusion are certain to be poor ones. Therefore, the new teacher would be wise to think about how she should react to a variety of problems before they occur.

The situations listed below eventually occur in all school situations. Student teachers and novices should consider these situations calmly before they arise and discuss them with their peers and supervisors if they are not confident of their ability to handle them properly. Thinking about them in advance will help the inexperienced educator to avoid panic when facing a totally unexpected situation. It will also let the new teacher know something about what she can look forward to encountering when she begins to work. Somehow, the pranks which seemed funny to us as students lose their humor when we become teachers. Overreacting or under-reacting are equally dangerous to the teacher's relationship with her pupils, peers and superiors. Before you are dependent upon your paycheck for the roof over your head and the food in the mouths of your children, calmly consider the following potential classroom problems to try to determine how you will handle them in a manner which is consistent with your own personality, with school policy and with the general welfare of your students.

1. A mother tells you that her son has not been attending his classes because larger boys have been extorting money from him and have threatened him with violence if he reports them or refuses to submit to their demands.

2. You and your students cannot concentrate on your lessons because the noise from the next classroom is consistently deafening. The teacher, you discover, is a veteran educator with fifteen years of experience with the system.

3. A fifteen-year-old student attends your after-school conference to tell you that he or she loves you desperately. Your initial reaction is to laugh at him but you know that this will hurt his feelings or invoke his anger.

4. A student who is failing tells you that he does not do his homework or study for tests because he must work to support his mother and sisters. His father is a heavy drinker who deserts the family periodically.

5. When you arrive at your classroom you find all your students picketing in front of your room refusing to attend class because they claim that you are irrelevant and unfair.

6. An irate parent accuses you of exhibiting racial prejudice in the grading of his child. He threatens to publicly expose you as a bigot.

7. A student you have never seen before opens your door while you are teaching, shouts obscenities into your room and runs away.

8. A student you have never seen before opens your door, shouts obscenities into your room and refuses to leave.

9. A pupil you have told to see you after school as a punishment for misbehavior does not report to you after you have reminded him to do so several times.

10. You discover that the classroom assigned to you is nothing more than a collection of chairs in a dreary fourth-floor hallway under leaky pipes and chipping paint and plaster.

11. You are a male teacher who has asked four female members of your class to stay after school to help you prepare a special project. The school is located in a high-crime area and before you realize it, it is dark out.

12. You want to take your students on a trip to a local industry for them to gather information for a report. Three students' parents refuse to give them permission.

13. You discover that the books assigned for your use are several grades above or below the ability levels of your students. Your book chairman informs you that they are the only texts he has available and you will just have to use them.

14. You assign the students to watch an educational program on television as the basis for a homework assignment. Two pupils tell you that they do not own televisions and another tells you that his father is the only one permitted to select the programs watched at night.

15. While you are teaching, most of your class gets up from their seats and begins to leave the room to join in a student protest against conditions in the school lunchroom.

16. Union membership in your school is very strong. A strike over salary increases has been called. Black teachers and parents have vowed to keep the schools opened at all costs. As a newcomer, you do not know enough about the issues to make an educated decision.

17. A student you have failed on his report card threatens to knife you if he ever sees you alone in the hallways or in the area around the school.

18. You must take the same public transportation to school that your pupils take. They take advantage of the crowded facilities to subject you to physical indignities and humiliation.

19. During your first semester at the school your department chairman or principal learns that you worked on the college newspaper and asks you to sponsor the school paper.

20. When you appear at the school for the first time you discover that you are scheduled to teach all slow classes.

21. Your department chairman consistently rates your performance in the classroom as inadequate. You honestly feel that you are doing a good job. His opinion prevents you from obtaining tenure and promotions.

22. During your first term you are asked to assume the responsibility of handling a student teacher. No one else in your department is willing to do it and you are the only one who has a schedule which meets university scheduling requirements.

23. You politely ask a student to stop his disruptive behavior in class and he shouts an obscenity at you in front of the entire class.

24. You are alone on lunchroom duty when thirty or forty students start throwing chairs at each other.

25. While patrolling the halls you detect the odor of marijuana emanating from the girls' lavatory. You enter and find six girls you don't know by name in the lavatory. None are smoking but there are three cigarettes in a toilet.

26. While you are on stairway duty, an intruder threatens to push you down the steps if you do not allow him to enter the building.

27. You think that three students in your room have cheated in a test but you cannot prove it.

28. You think that three students have cheated in a test and you can prove it.

29. You discover that a student in your senior college preparatory class has plagiarized his term paper. If he does not maintain his A average in your class, he will lose his scholarship.

30. You have been asked to take over a senior honors section in the middle of the semester when their teacher leaves the system suddenly. You do not feel qualified to handle the course.

31. During your free period you are told to substitute for a teacher who has suddenly become ill. You have no lesson plans or seating charts for this course.

32. One student in your class is constantly asking you questions which are not relevant to the subject under discussion. If you do not call on him he waves his hand wildly or calls out.

33. A bright student with a nervous disorder cannot seem to refrain from humming or tapping on his desk while you are teaching. You have spoken to him about it and he honestly tells you he doesn't even realize that he's doing it.

34. You are eavesdropping on a student's conversation with her girlfriend during lunchroom duty and you learn that the girl is trying to obtain an illegal abortion.

35. Before you can disperse a crowd at the window, someone drops a small metal file cabinet out of the window. A passer-by is injured. You do not know which student dropped the cabinet.

Epilogue

The examples of the type of difficulties teachers routinely face given in the last chapter should scare away all those who do not have the courage, strength and dedication to become good teachers. The professionals who remain have the potential for becoming outstanding educators. Few good teachers are born that way. Most are developed after several terms of disappointments, depression, dejection, exhaustion and moments of excitement and exhilaration. Try to bear in mind that the first few years are the most difficult. As you gain more experience in your profession the irritations decrease, the exhaustion diminishes and the satisfaction soars.

A teacher is very much like a physician. Once she enters her profession, she can no longer separate her personal life from her professional life. She relates almost every part of her private life to her school life unconsciously. She begins taking placemats from restaurants because they contain puzzles which will stimulate her slow learners. She invites her folk-singing friends to come to her class to stimulate their thoughts about political issues or old English ballads. The newspaper articles, journals and magazines she reads are related to what she is teaching or what Johnny Jones was asking her about last week. When the garage mechanic tells her he can't repair her car immediately because his assistant quit, she remembers the boy in her trade course who needed extra money to help his family. And when she checks the Sunday paper for the week's television listings she looks not only for her own favorites but for programs relevant to her students' studies. Finally, she discovers that she begins reading the books and magazines, listening to the radio stations and viewing the television programs her pupils seem to enjoy so that she can become more aware of what they enjoy and what they can relate to. Eventually, she discovers that her language has changed to include some of the intonational patterns and expressions commonly used by her classes. As she affects and alters the lives of her pupils, so they contribute to her growth and awareness.

More teacher dropouts occur during and immediately after the first year of teaching. Those who have the physical, emotional and mental stamina to return to school after their first summer vacation find that they are entrenched in a rewarding, exciting career. Most assuredly, the initial year in the classroom is physically and emotional trying. New teachers need the understanding and support of their families who will have to put up with their grouchy moods, crying sessions and periods of prolonged silence. But if the teacher can survive the first-year "indoctrination of fire" she is "home free." As the years progress, the good, warm, satisfying moments increase and the times of stress decrease. The latter never disappear entirely. It would be too much to hope for this in any profession. But, as with giving birth to a child, the mind quickly blocks out the painful moments and remembers only the beautiful times. Teachers who can look back on years of experience in the classroom can tell you many stories about the college students who come back after graduation to thank them for the positive influences they exterted on their lives, about the smiles of the slow learners who get their first 100% on a test, about the gratitude of the boy they helped place in a job and about the excitement of students who hear themselves on tape or present a program to the student body or have a short story published in the school magazine for the first time. These reminiscences far outnumber the stories about the fires set in the boys' gymnasium during the final examination period, the tires and vinyl roofs slashed in the faculty parking lot, and the "stink bombs" planted in the ventilating systems.

Experienced, successful teachers are rarely bored and infrequently lonely. They lead exciting, stimulating lives full of the rich feeling of contributing to the total growth of other human beings and to society as a whole. This warm feeling is well worth the 130 papers a teacher grades a week, the 25 lessons she plans a week and the 157 dirty milk cartons she clears off of the lunchroom tables after the pupils have left. Few people have as great an opportunity to influence the course of society as a teacher does. And few people carry as great a responsibility.

Index

Absence from school
  students, 45, 84, 112, 142, 199
  teachers, 45, 84, 192, 193
Advanced placement courses, 229
Attendance
  recording of, 131, 150-152
  students, 18, 199

Blackboards, 28, 110
"Black English," 201
Book boys, 45-46
Bulletin boards, 27, 79, 87-91, 98, 135, 225

Classroom regulations, 109-110
Club sponsorship, 135, 154-155
Computers, 175, 227
Conferences
  with pupils, 28, 35-36, 48, 57, 95, 103, 142-143
  with parents, 64, 137-138, 175, 200-201, 221, 222-223
Contraband, 59-60, 61
Cumulative records, 106-107
Curriculum changes, 68-69, 120-121, 126
Custodians, 156-157, 119

Department chairman, 15, 28, 125, 130, 133-137, 139
Diagnostic tests, 21-22, 37, 106, 164
Directed Reading Activities (DRA), 99-104
Discipline, 17, 33, 55-65
Dress regulations, 47, 49, 51
Drugs, 62

Essay tests, 61-63
Extra-credit assignments, 170-171
Extracurricular duties, 135, 149-155

Faculty meetings, 121, 136
Fire drills, 29, 84

Gangs, 144-145, 202
Grade keeping, 131, 173-176
Guards, 193-194
Guest speakers, 76-77

Home-Community Coordinators, 220
Home visitations, 139-149, 223
Homeroom, 149-153
Homework, 28, 46, 81-83, 110-112, 113

Individually Prescribed Program (IPI), 232-235
Instructional Media Center, 224-225

Lateness, 18, 60-61, 199-200
Lay readers, 155-156
Lesson Plans, 14, 67-85, 112, 115, 131, 133

Magnet schools, 229-230
Medical services, 36-37, 62, 183, 184-187, 192, 212
Mini-courses, 223-224
Modular scheduling, 224
Money collections, 153
Motivation, 38, 67, 75-76, 108

Objective tests, 163-164
Observations
of peers, 126-127
of you, 28, 84, 134
Open classroom, 229-230
Oral reading, 101-102
Oral tests, 160-161

Parent-Teacher's Association, (PTA), 188
Parent's night, 137-138, 200
Preclass work, 73-75
Protest demonstrations, 145-147

Report cards, 137-138, 172, 174-176
Rural education, 197, 211-215, 230-231

Seating charts, 15-16, 34-35
Secretaries, 156

Student teachers, 129-132
Substitute teachers, 15, 45, 84
Supplies, 41-42
care of, 29, 44
distribution of, 26-27, 29, 44-46
sharing of, 72, 123

Team teaching, 38, 125-126
Television, 225-226
Testing days, 47
Trips, 78, 116
Truancy, 151
Tutors, 96, 188

Unions, 127-128, 194

Vestibule classes, 228-229

Weapons, 144